LACE
FANS

ANN COLLIER

B T BATSFORD · LONDON

Figure 1: Twelve Days of Christmas fan worked in needlelace and applied to mauve net mounted on antique mother-of-pearl sticks. I have included all the figures to correspond with the song: 12 pipers piping, 11 drummers drumming, 10 Lords a-leaping, 9 ladies dancing, 8 maids a-milking, 7 swans a-swimming, 6 geese a-laying, 5 gold rings, 4 calling birds, 3 French hens, 2 turtle doves and a partridge in a pear tree.

Text and original designs © Ann Collier 2002
The moral right of the author has been asserted.

First Published 2002
for the publishers

B T Batsford
64 Brewery Road
London N7 9NT

www.batsford.com

A member of **Chrysalis** Books plc

A CIP catalogue record for this book is available from the British Library.

ISBN 07134 8734 8

Printed in Spain

CONTENTS

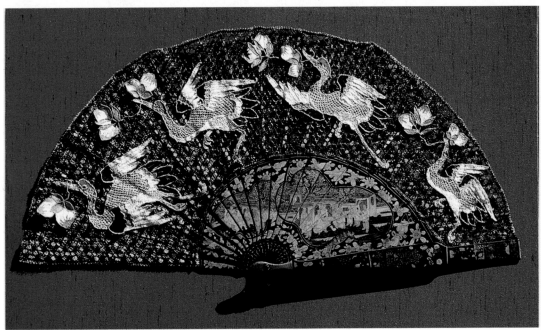

Figures 2 and 3: Double-sided Cranes fan (see page 9 for more details).

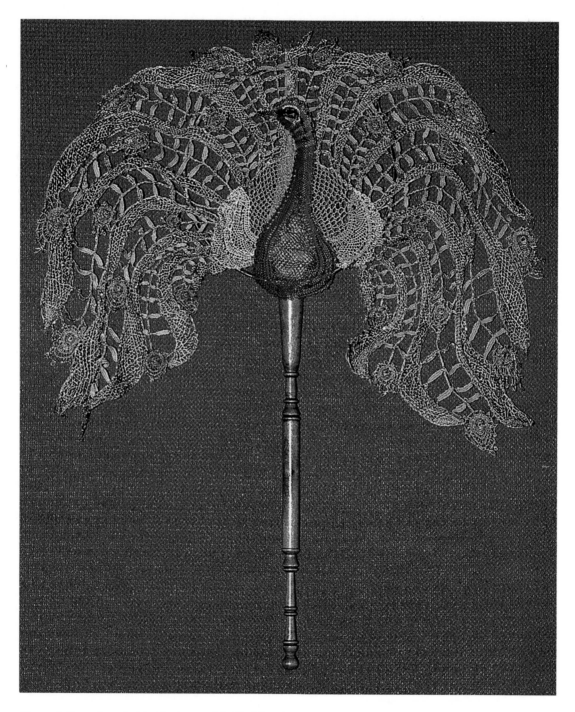

Figure 4: Peacock worked in Honiton and Bedfordshire lace techniques (see page 9 for more details).

INTRODUCTION

Fans have probably existed since man first inhabited the earth and used a palm leaf to keep cool in a hot climate.

They were used for winnowing grain and carried in ceremonial processions by many ancient civilizations. The Chinese and Japanese have the longest continuous history – they used fans in court etiquette and theatrical productions. It is said that it was they who invented the folding fan by observing the way a bat folded its wings.

Fans were gradually introduced into Europe through trade with the East and became an essential fashion accessory by the 17th century, especially in the warm climates of Italy, Spain and France.

By the 18th century, fans were in common use throughout Europe and were often designed to show the wealth of the owner – the leaves were painted by famous artists and the sticks encrusted with precious stones and gold leaf.

Scenes on the leaf were historical or mythological and were often painted in a rectangle, a piece being then cut out to accommodate the fan sticks.

By the late 18th century the leaf was custom-made to fit the sticks, with designs set in areas and surrounded by a painted border. The sticks were designed to match the leaf.

Historical events were very popular on Georgian fans, including images of battles (Waterloo), balloonists' first flight, coronations and so forth.

When the printing of pictures became possible, printed fans were very popular and inexpensive; slogans, cartoons, riddles and commemorative and political themes all had their place.

Fans were an indispensable part of costume: a lady needed something to hold and, as can be seen from the Language of the Fan (page 120), it was a great means of communication. The size of the fan changed with each decade and seemed to increase or decrease in proportion to the ground area covered by women's skirts: small fans in the early 1800s and larger fans in the 1850s.

Shapes, too, changed with fashion: early fans in 1600 were only quarter-circles, changing gradually to half-circles by the 18th century; ellipses came in with the Art Nouveau movement in the late 19th century.

Lace was very fashionable and expensive from the 16th century but lace fans were rare until the 19th century, when they were made in abundance using every technique of lacemaking. Those that exist today usually date from 1820 to 1910, when they were extremely popular. As these fans were usually highly patterned, they complemented the colourful dresses of the period and were generally mounted on plain sticks of mother-of-pearl, abalone shell or bone.

The leaves were made to fit the sticks and, though the pieces were made as a cottage industry, particularly in England, they were assembled professionally. The cheaper leaves were made in a simple design, usually floral, but beautiful expensive Chantilly ones often had scenes on them in much the same way as the painted ones.

Six different lacemaking techniques are commonly found on fans. Those that were custom-made have a detailed upper edge and lower edge, a design on one guard stick and an extra piece to accommodate the other guard stick.

If a fan leaf has a turned-back area stuck to the guard sticks, then it was probably made from another piece of lace, such as a collar or a deep edge.

The names of the types of laces correspond to the towns or areas in which they were made.

NEEDLELACE

This is constructed buttonhole stitch upon buttonhole stitch, with a needle and thread on a pre-couched framework. Fans were made in Belgium (Point de Gaze), France (Alençon), Ireland (Youghal) and Italy (Point de Venise), and all had their own distinctive characteristics, some of the stitches being copyrighted.

BOBBIN LACE

This is constructed on a hard pillow with thread wound on to bobbins. The threads are twisted or plaited and pinned into place.

Fans were made in Chantilly, Valenciennes and Blonde (France), Duchesse (Belgium), Bedfordshire, Buckinghamshire and Honiton (England) and Malta.

Bedfordshire and Maltese lace have a ground of wheat ears and plaits instead of a net.

Bucks, Chantilly and *Blonde* have a twisted net

ground with motifs outlined in a thicker thread (gimp).

Torchon consists of simple geometric shapes on a closed pin ground and is made in many countries.

Honiton and Duchesse are composed of motifs with the use of sewings to join parts together.

Milanese is a bobbin-lace braid in tape-like form which can be decorated with fancy open areas worked in it. It takes few bobbins and with the use of 'sewings' as in Honiton, large areas can be worked.

NEEDLERUN OR LIMERICK LACE

This is decorated machine net with darning in a variety of patterns. The technique probably came from France but was introduced and taught in Ireland by nuns in the convent in Limerick. It was sold to generate funds for the poor in Ireland following the potato famine. It was a great success and was patronised by royalty. Fans in this lace would date from 1840.

CARRICKMACROSS

This is lawn or other semi-transparent material applied to machine net and sometimes decorated with Limerick fillings. It was introduced into Ireland during the potato famine so these fans would again date from 1840 onwards.

TENERIFE

This was constructed on a circle of pins on a metal wheel, attached to a hard pillow. Threads were stretched across from pin to pin in spoke formation and held in place by stitches and simple weaving.

It was made, as the name implies, in the Canary Islands but also in Paraguay, Brazil and Mexico. The technique originally came from Spain.

TAPE LACE

This is sometimes called Branscombe point after the small Devon town where it was made in the 1860s. It consists of a woven tape tacked down to form a pattern and the spaces filled with needlelace stitches. Not to be confused with Milanese.

Fans are half-circles or slightly less, sometimes quarter-circles and occasionally half an ellipse. A good lace fan must have the lace custom-made to fit the fan sticks; if the design on the sticks matches the lace so much the better. It is important to have the sticks to hand before designing the lace, although a few makers of sticks will make them to fit the lace.

Because lace is delicate and decorative and takes time and skill to create, it deserves to be mounted on beautiful sticks. Wood is often too heavy but looks fine on large fans.

Some antique fans are found with ebony sticks but more usual materials are bone, ivory, mother-of-pearl or tortoiseshell. It is therefore worth looking around for antique sticks with damaged leaves. These sticks are not usually sought after by collectors. Badly broken sticks are not ideal but if the guards are in good condition, it is possible to repair or remove the damaged inners and re-rivet the sticks.

CLEANING AND MENDING

Never wash sticks. Bone absorbs water and discolours; wood and tortoiseshell warp and mother-of-pearl falls into pieces as the glue dissolves.

Some silicon polishes do the job well. Use a soft cloth and take great care as some old sticks are very brittle and break easily. Use one of the instant adhesives to repair the broken parts. If a stick is badly fractured, it may be necessary to remove it, glue it to an adjacent stick or reinforce it with a sliver of the same material.

Carved ivory is more difficult to clean: the delicate carving often has decades of dust and dirt in its crevices. A cotton bud soaked in lemon juice helps to remove this and will bleach the ivory slightly. Wash out carefully, but dry quickly with a hair dryer.

Figures 2 and 3 (page 6): Double-sided Cranes fan. The antique Chinese lacquer sticks are very unusual, being asymmetrical. They are double-sided with different gold paintings on either side. I decided to work cranes with peach blossom in their beaks as this represents long life and happiness. On one side the cranes are in coloured needlelace on a background of black bobbin lace and on the other the birds are in black bobbin lace on a gold bobbin lace background. This is effectively two fans in one.

Figure 4 (page 7): Peacock worked in Honiton and Bedfordshire lace techniques. The tail is wired and the whole is mounted on a turned stick. The body and wings are worked in Honiton techniques with the tail in a mixture of Bedfordshire plaits and leaves. These combine with circles or ovals worked in Bruges lace techniques (turning on a central pin).

Figure 5: The Millennium. This is worked in needlelace on a bobbin lace background. I placed the Maoris in front of the sunrise as they are the first to greet it, and the rest of the world standing together as a crowd. This was made to celebrate the turn of the century and I decided to put all the various people of the world together in a friendly situation. You will see a Jew with his arms around Arabs and an Irish Orangeman with his arms around an Irish dancer. I used John Lennon's 'Imagine' and wrote a verse on the sticks.

Figure 6: An Egyptian Chase. This is worked in Bedfordshire bobbin lace using some colour. It depicts a hunt scene when all the family went out together. Father is the largest figure and regarded as the most important, Mother is very small, as are the children. Son is, however, a little larger. Even the cat is taken along to flush out the birds. They are in typical Ancient Egyptian dress. The idea came from tomb paintings and was an experiment to try Bedfordshire lace in several colours by using coloured weavers for the solid parts with cream passives. The hieroglyphics spell 'Ann Collier' and are worked in needlelace.

CHAPTER 1
DESIGNING FANS IN BOBBIN LACE

Design in fans has always been very varied; picture books of antique fans give ideas and can sometimes be adapted. Lace, however, needs special organisation.

Torchon is the easiest to design as it has regular geometric shapes that can be worked out on graph paper and, for fan purposes, on polar graph paper which gives a curved movement to the ground.

PREPARATION
Fan sticks come in many sizes and the shape of the fan leaf must be constructed to fit them.

1. Spread the sticks out to form a semi-circle as evenly as possible on tracing paper.
2. Mark in the inner circle and the outer circle and remove the sticks. Check these lines by placing over polar graph paper and correct if necessary.
3. Mark in these lines on to the graph paper and plot in a dotted grid.

4. Use this to draw geometric patterns and, when a satisfactory one is decided upon, mark in a suitable top and bottom edge and trace the complete design on to the original traced shape.
5. Mark in all the dots and it is ready for working.

The final design was marked out with crossed trails and squares of rose ground and half stitch. The lower band was designed with leaves and plaits. It was tried again in black with colour added and the pattern enlarged to 140 per cent.

Many people will remark that these Torchon designs can be worked out on a computer, which makes the designs more accurate but they are very rigid especially when designing for Floral Bucks or Torchon. I prefer designs worked out with a more artistic approach and not controlled by a machine. Hand-made lace has a certain element of irregularity which sets it apart from the machine made and it is my opinion that we should keep it that way.

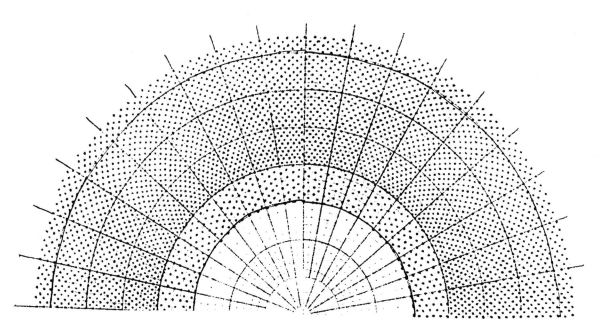

Diagram 1: Dotted polar graph paper.

Diagram 2: Pattern drawn out on polar graph paper.

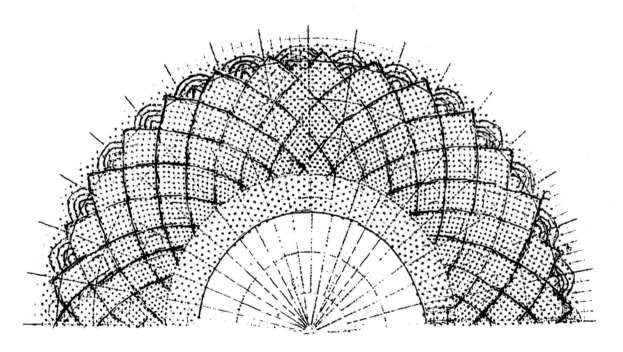

Diagram 3: An alternative pattern drawn out on polar graph paper.

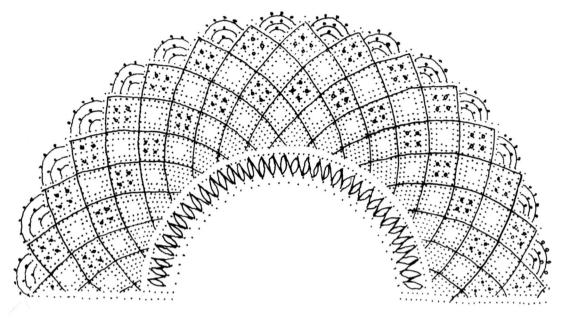

Diagram 4: Pattern ready for working (see also diagram 20, page 49).

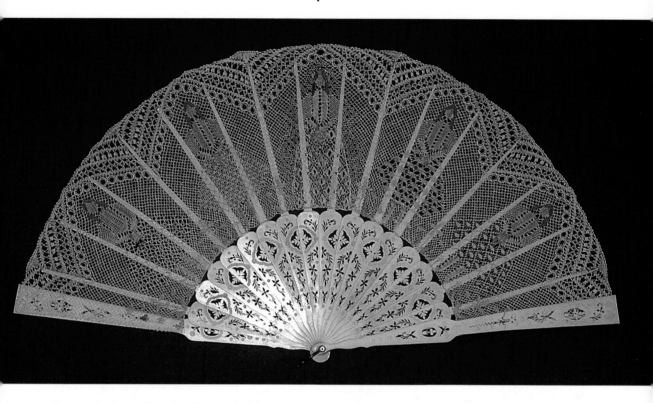

Figure 7 (left): Small Torchon fans worked from diagram 4.

Figure 8 (above): Bride and Bridesmaids fan.

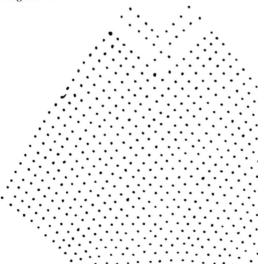

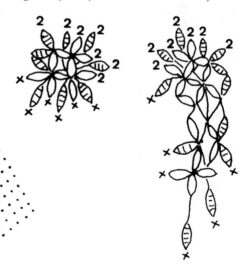

Diagram 5c: Dress pattern for personal design.

Diagram 5d: Bride bouquets worked in Bedfordshire leaves and plaits.

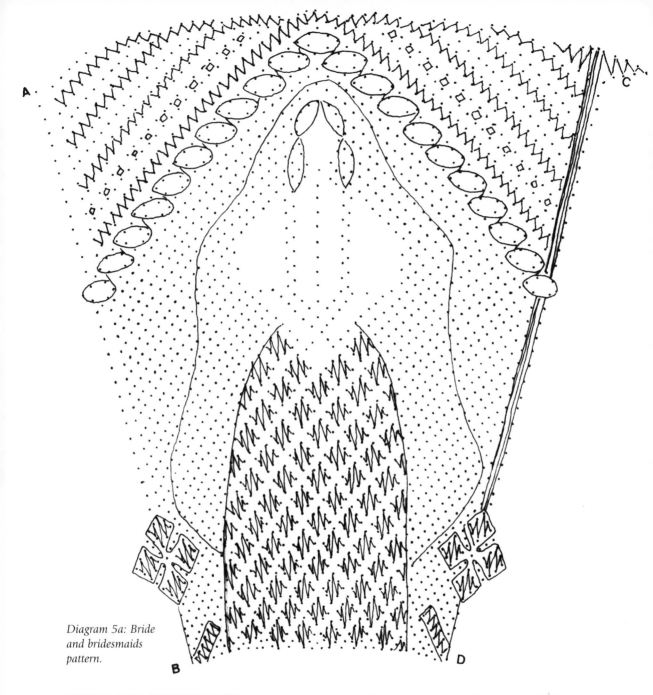

A

C

B

D

Diagram 5a: Bride and bridesmaids pattern.

BRIDE AND BRIDESMAIDS

Materials: Approx 80 pairs 30 DMC, and several gimps in perlé 8.

This design was worked out as before on marked polar graph paper. The curved ground line can be clearly seen and has been exploited to create the curved arches under which the figures stand. A limited amount of colour was used for the hair, bridesmaids' bodices and for the bouquets and the flowers at the base, but it can look just as effective without. The bride is central, with two bridesmaids on either side.

To make the pattern, match each section to the next, matching the arches and the lower flowers and joining AB to AB and CD to CD, reversing the bridesmaids each time. I have changed the bride dress from the original to make it more solid and one can add spots to the veil. There is a simple spare

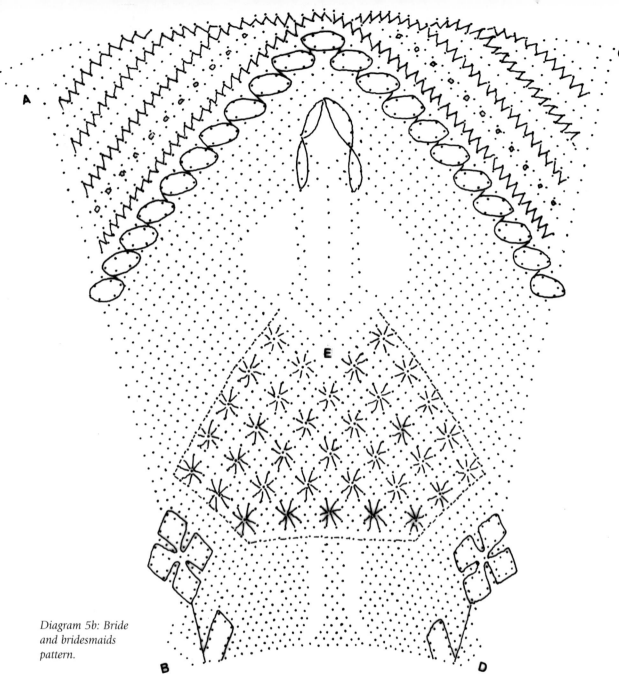

Diagram 5b: Bride and bridesmaids pattern.

dress pattern (diagram 5c) that can be inserted so that you can make each bridesmaid's dress different, using different filling stitches of your own choice.

Start on the arch surrounding a bridesmaid CD and work following the curved ground lines. The hair consists of leaves which start at the shoulder, worked over the head to the other shoulder. These are made first and the face worked over the top.

Sleeves are in half stitch with cloth stitch for face, arms, body and legs, and different Torchon fillings for the skirts.

Work the bouquets from diagram 5d when the fan is finished. Make leaves as shown, with two pairs for each, one pink and one green so that the weaver can change for flower petal or leaf. Plaits link it together until they finally tie out where shown at X. Attach to the solid block of cloth stitch where the arms meet and sew the ends through to the wrong side.

BUCKS DESIGN ON
POLAR GRAPH PAPER

Materials: Approx 88 pairs DMC 60, and several gimps in perlé 12

This design was formed by taking two antique edge prickings from Luton Museum and positioning them on to the lower and upper edges of the fan shape to form a pleasing arrangement. The ground was plotted in from pre-marked polar graph paper and the areas of point ground and honeycomb filled in.

You will notice that using polar graph paper means that the ground flows easily on the curved lines. The ground at the base is smaller than that at the top and the angle changes. At the top it is 45 degrees and at the bottom closer to 60.

To the purist Bucks worker this is not satisfactory, but I find it works well in most cases. An alternative method is to use the Bucks hexagon as shown on page 22.

Make the complete pattern by reversing and joining at DE. Start at A, adding pairs from A to B and work in the direction shown by the arrows. All the pairs will be on from B to C. Continue to add pairs if necessary to keep the cloth areas firm. Finish as you began at AB, cutting off the threads as they accumulate. Remember that this edge lies under a guard stick.

Diagram 6a (above): Edge patterns from Luton Museum used in the fan pattern.
Figure 9 (below): Small Bucks fan. This is worked from diagram 6 a and b.

Figure 10: Bucks fan worked in black and gold from diagram 7.

BUCKS DESIGN IN BLACK AND GOLD

Materials: 78 pairs DMC 60 in black, and several gimps in gold.

This is a continuous edge pattern adapted from an antique handkerchief edge in Blonde lace and because it is in black, the solid parts are in half stitch. Each flower has two solid petals and open honeycomb rings for the others, with a gold gimp used throughout.

Reverse the pattern DE and join at the centre. Start at A and work from A to B and from A to C simultaneously, following the curved ground lines. Point ground and honeycomb have been used throughout.

Finish at AB, cutting off pairs as they accumulate and still following the ring edge.

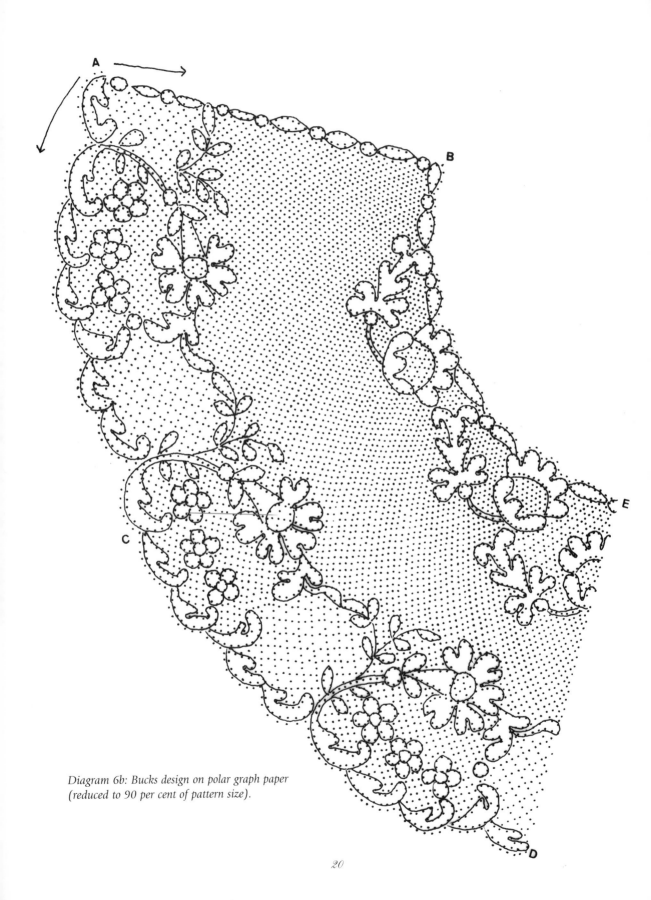

Diagram 6b: Bucks design on polar graph paper (reduced to 90 per cent of pattern size).

Diagram 7: Bucks design in black and gold (reduced to 90 per cent of pattern size).

DESIGNING BUCKS FANS USING THE HEXAGON FORMAT

Hexagon format is made by dotting out isometric paper (60) to make a Bucks ground.

1. Start with a honeycomb ring on the 60 ground.
2. Mark in the rows of dots that radiate from it; these can be extended to the required size of fan.
3. Position the open fan on the paper so that the fan rivet is on the honeycomb ring. Draw in the fan leaf shape, lower and upper edges.
4. Mark in the break points.
5. Spread the open fan sticks on to tracing paper and again draw in the fan leaf.
6. Plan the design within this shape, bearing in mind the upper and lower edges and the break lines (where the ground changes direction), also where the fancy filling will be.
7. Place the finished design on to the hexagon paper and plot the dots. Mark the break lines.

   This format makes an even Bucks ground but because one is fitting a half-circle into a hexagon, pairs will accumulate on the top and bottom edges.

I learnt many years ago that when working Floral Bucks or Beds, one adds pairs and takes out pairs where necessary, unlike Torchon or geometric Bucks.

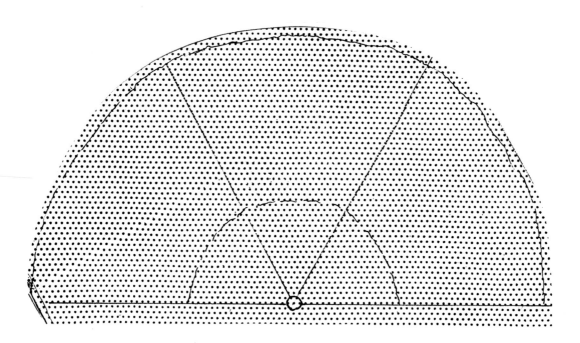

Diagram 8: Plotting a hexagon format

Figure 11: Large Bucks fan with design taken from an antique lappet. It is worked from diagram 9 a, b and c.

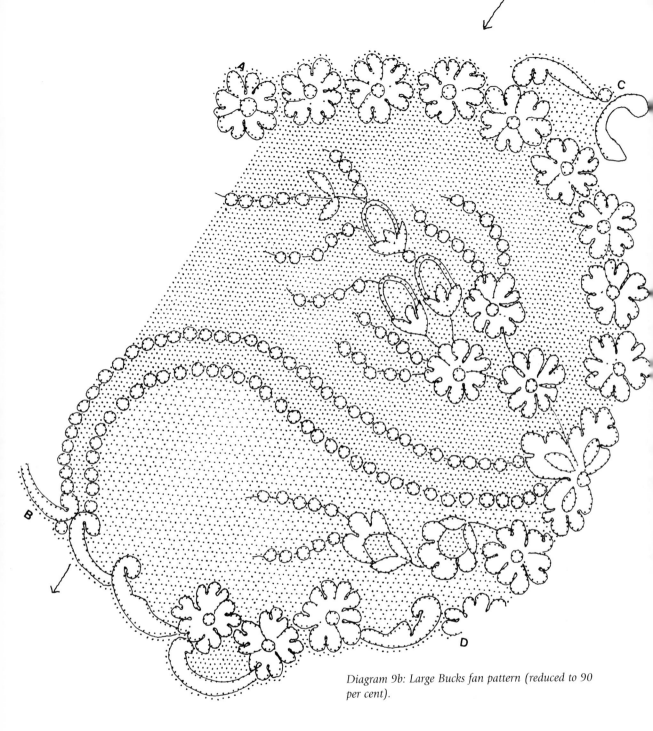

Diagram 9b: Large Bucks fan pattern (reduced to 90 per cent).

BUCKS FAN PATTERN USING THE HEXAGON FORMAT

Materials: Approx 230 pairs 80 Cotona, and several gimps in perlé 12

This large fan was designed from an antique lappet. The break points are planned to occur at the arc of flowers and in the centre.

To make the pattern, join the three pieces AB to AB

C

E

D

F

Diagram 9a: Large Bucks fan pattern (reduced to 90 per cent).

and CD to CD, then reverse the whole pattern matching at the centre EF.

Begin at G and work in the direction of the arrows C.

Work up to and including the arc of flowers. This is the break line and a change of direction (see arrow). Work in the direction indicated to the centre. Change direction until the arc of flowers is complete on the second side, then change direction to the

finish. Pairs can be removed and added again where necessary and all will be removed at the end. You are working on the wrong side so that this finish will lie under the guard stick and the start edge will be the one that shows on top of the other guard stick.

This is not an easy pattern with the large number of bobbins involved but all the techniques are Bucks and a competent Floral Bucks lacemaker will find it a challenge.

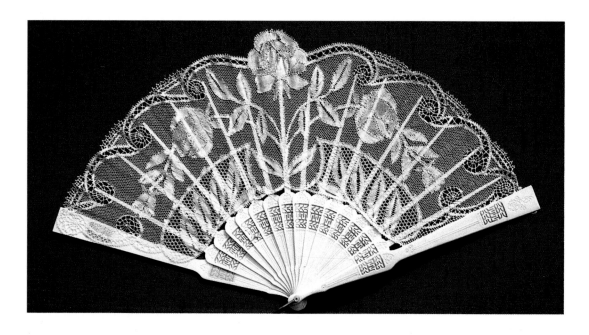

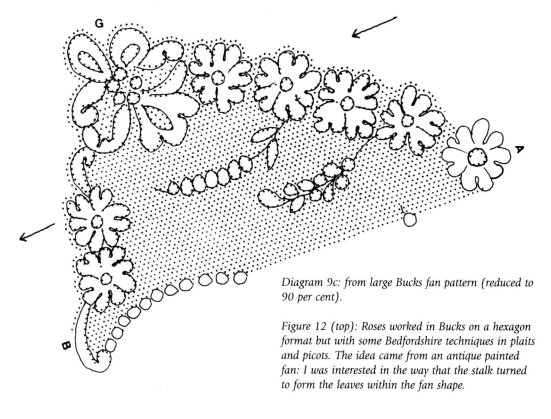

Diagram 9c: from large Bucks fan pattern (reduced to 90 per cent).

Figure 12 (top): Roses worked in Bucks on a hexagon format but with some Bedfordshire techniques in plaits and picots. The idea came from an antique painted fan: I was interested in the way that the stalk turned to form the leaves within the fan shape.

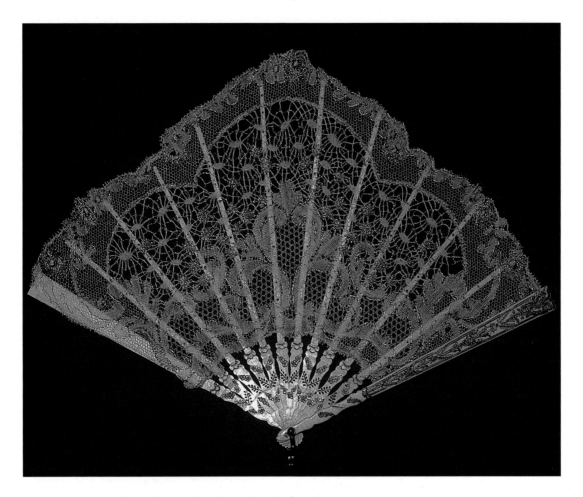

Figure 13: Art Deco fan worked with spiders and circles from diagram 10.

ART DECO BUCKS/TORCHON FAN

Materials: Approx 180 pairs DMC 60, gold gimp and several gold pairs in Madeira 40

This is worked on the hexagon format using only two sections so that the break line is central. Reverse BC to form the pattern. It is an Art Deco shape and only a quarter-circle.

Begin at A and work in the direction of the arrows. The Torchon spiders are surrounded by a plait that divides in to two and surrounds each spider. The plain circles are worked in cloth stitch with a gold weaver. Some of the flowers are in gold, others in cream and the flower centres are tallies.

The outer edges are worked in Floral Bucks but the central panel is a mixture of cloth stitch circles with gold weavers and Torchon spiders.

These spiders have two pairs in a plait to start off the circle, with single pairs coming in to work the spider body. They return out to the circle again and the surround joins to form a plait for the next spider ring or woven circle.

If carefully controlled, it is possible to use a gold plait to divide for the surround, joining at the end of the spider and used either for another surround or as the weavers in a cloth stitch circle.

Diagram 10: Bucks/Torchon pattern with rings and spiders (reduced to 90 per cent).

THE ROWAN TREE IN BEDFORDSHIRE TECHNIQUES

Materials: Approx 180 pairs 80 Cotona and short lengths of gimp perlé 12 or DMC 30.

This is another Art Deco shape and was an experiment to use a wide variety of grounds that are to be found in Thomas Lester designs of the 19th century.

My design is based on the rowan tree with its leaves, flowers and berries. It was worked out on polar graph paper so that the threads would follow through. This is not an easy design but Floral Bedfordshire lacemakers should have no difficulty.

Make the pattern by joining AB to AB, matching the leaves in the central spray. Begin at CD with a woven trail, adding pairs where necessary.

TOP

Double ninepin edge with leaf tallies at intervals. Crossed trails with a raised tally at the crossing; see diagram 12.

Rowan flowers in cloth stitch, berries with a raised tally in the centre.

Rowan leaves are worked in cloth stitch, weavers meeting at the centre vein with a gimp surround. The ground is a two-plait crossing; see diagram 11b.

BOTTOM

This consists of woven flowers with a plait crossing in the centre, alternating with wheels as in diagram 13.

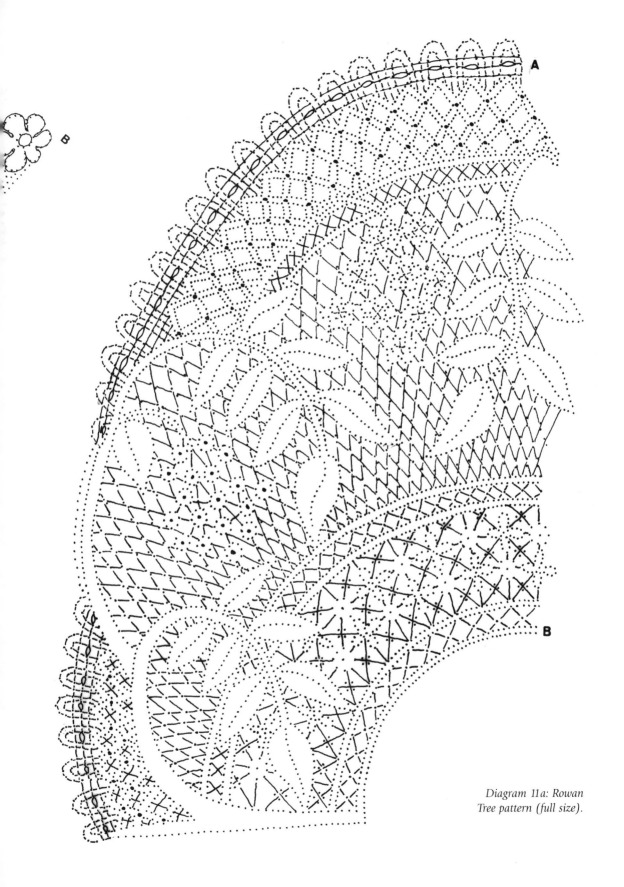

Diagram 11a: Rowan Tree pattern (full size).

*Figure 14: Rowan Tree worked in Bedfordshire
techniques as in Thomas Lester lace. See diagram
11 a, b and c.*

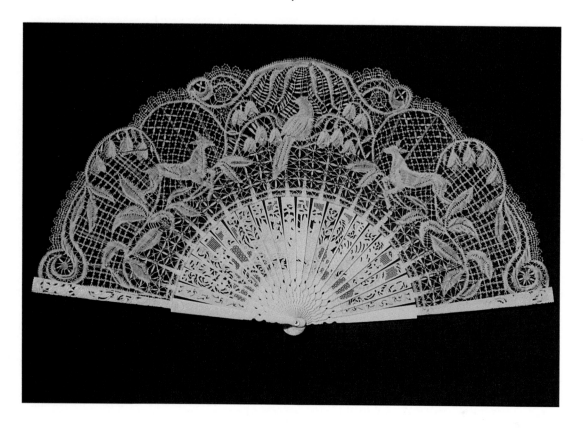

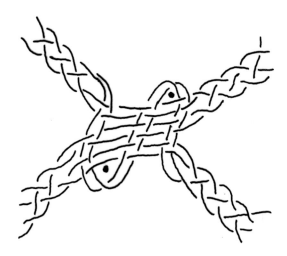

Figure 15: The Umbrella Tree. This was worked in Thomas Lester type Bedfordshire bobbin lace. I have used a variety of filling stitches and have added extra bobbin-lace petals to the bell flowers and an extra wing on the bird. The double plait ground gives the necessary extra pairs for working the deer. Many years ago I photographed some lace in the Cecil Higgins Museum in Bedford. The grounds that I used were copied from these enlarged photographs.

Diagram 11b: Double plait crossing.

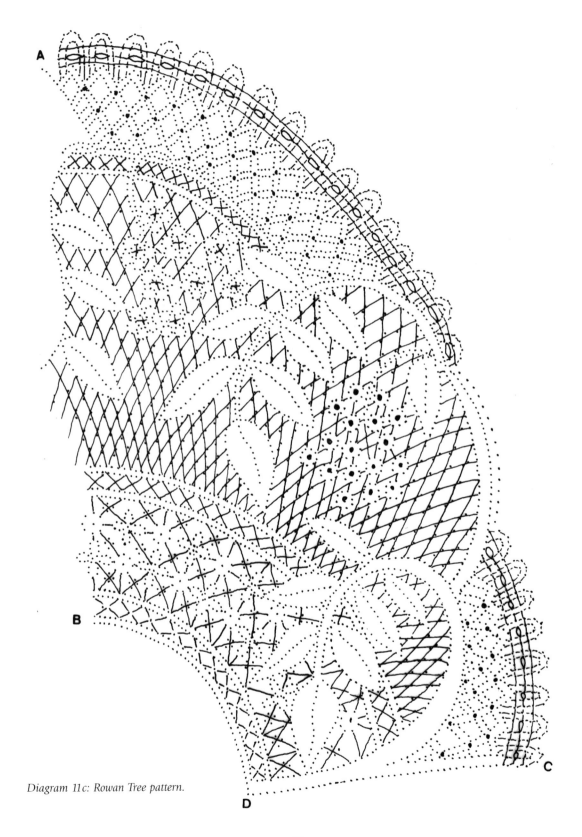

A

B

D

C

Diagram 11c: Rowan Tree pattern.

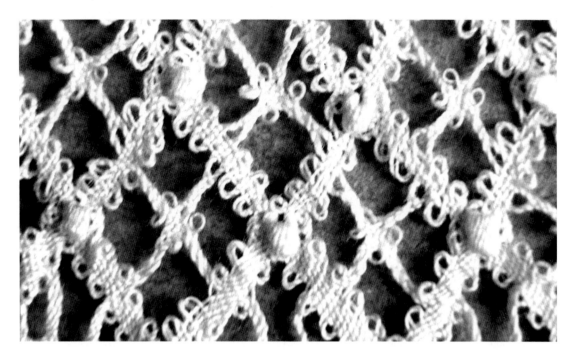

Diagram 12 (above): Crossed trails with raised tallies.

Diagram 13 (below): Woven flowers and plaited wheels.

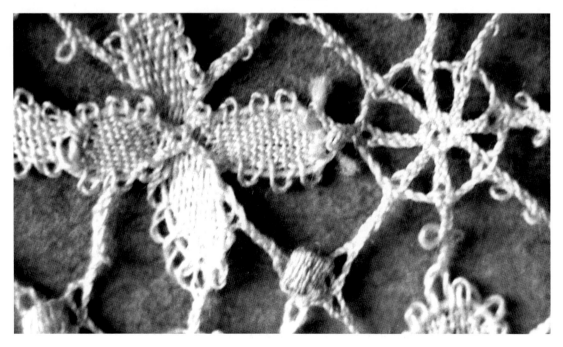

Figure 16 (above): The Chase. This idea was taken from the carved design on the sticks, which depicted a hunting scene. Worked in Bedfordshire lace techniques using various grounds and dark cream weavers for the figures and the animals. The men with spears are chasing deer and the dog is chasing the rabbits. The lower panel has a variety of fish worked in Buckinghamshire lace techniques. The fan is mounted on antique carved ivory sticks.

Figure 17 (top right): Roses. These were worked in Bedfordshire bobbin lace with extra petals on the flowers, which have small gold beads added for stamens. The idea came from an old Thomas Lester pricking; see diagram 14.

Figure 18 (bottom right): Bookmark fan. This was made from my Bedfordshire practice pieces designed by Barbara Underwood. Any bookmark can be organised into a fan shape; see diagram 15.

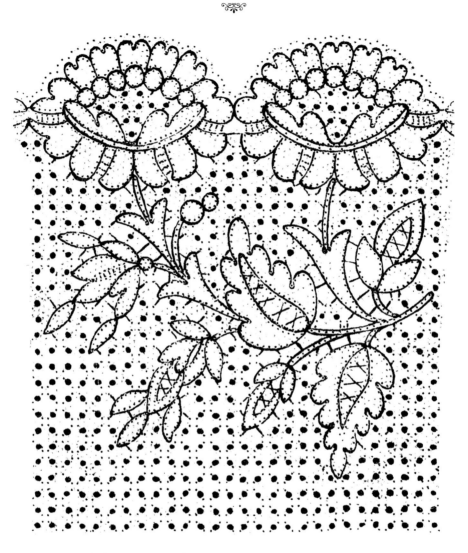

Diagram 14: Roses: an old Thomas Lester pricking.

BOOKMARK FAN

Many of us make bookmarks, especially when we are learning, as they require few bobbins. I have never found a use for them and they tend to be put away and forgotten. When I was learning Floral Bedfordshire I made several to try out leaves, raised tallies and picot ground, and I finally decided to make them into a fan.

I spaced them at intervals to fit some sticks and worked out an infill of Beds leaves and plaits with picots. As most bookmarks end in a tassel, I decided

to leave out pairs as I approached the point and then form these into a half-spider and fasten off. Another alternative is to carry on the centre two pairs of the infill, make another leaf and join this to another set of leaves that can form the lower edge. This method could be used for bookmarks in any lace technique, Torchon, Bucks or Beds.

This infill takes 16 pairs with four pairs used first for the top trail from A to B, adding the other pairs as indicated. At the end of the trail at B, the four pairs are then used to work the plaits at B.

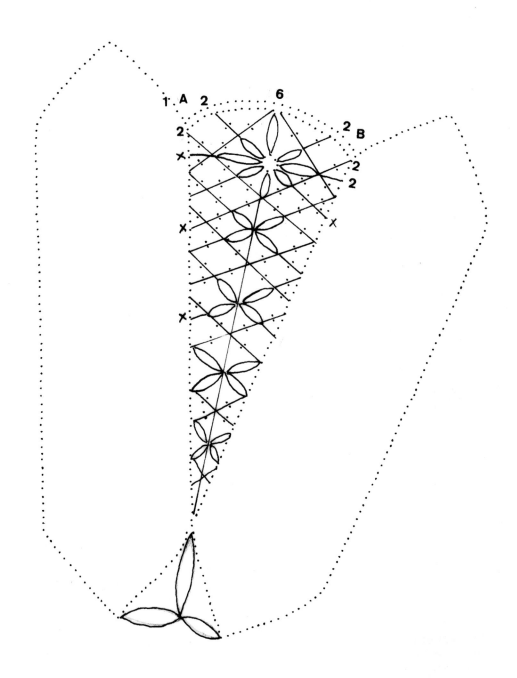

Diagram 15: Bookmark fan.

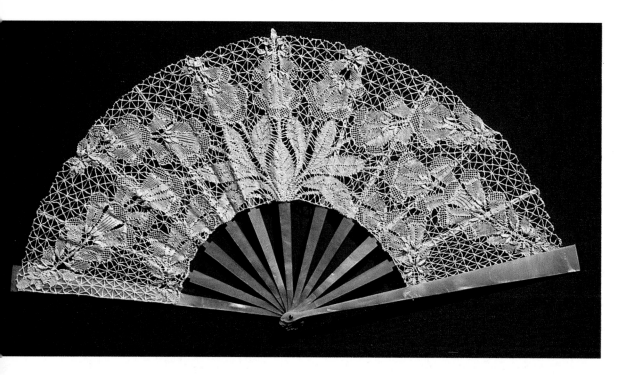

Figure 19 (above): Foxgloves (see also page 42).   *Figure 20 (below): Painted roses (see also page 42).*

Figure 21: Briar roses painted and worked as in diagram 16.

EDGES TO PAINTED FANS

Lace edges to fans are very common on antique pieces. This is much quicker than making a whole fan and can be made to fit sticks of any size.

A shaped edge makes the fan more interesting.
Materials: 46 pairs (approx) 50 or 60 DMC with Sylko perlé 12 for gimps.
To make the pattern, join A to A and reverse from B.

Continue the gimp ringed edge for the required length of side and lower edge.

Start at B and work in the direction of the arrows, adding pairs on both sides when needed. It will be necessary with the changing size of the edge to take out pairs as they accumulate and add them again later. When worked in one piece, the pairs that end with leaves at A can be carried on for the corner piece. Continue with the pairs, working the ringed edge for the required length to the other side when pairs are again added to continue. Finish at B as neatly as possible.

Make the leaf in silk taffeta to give stiffness and cut it to the size of the sticks.

I have included some painting ideas, which can be arranged to suit. I use acrylic paints and shade the flowers and leaves. The design can be copied on to the silk using a soft pencil and the lace attached with four-sided stitch.

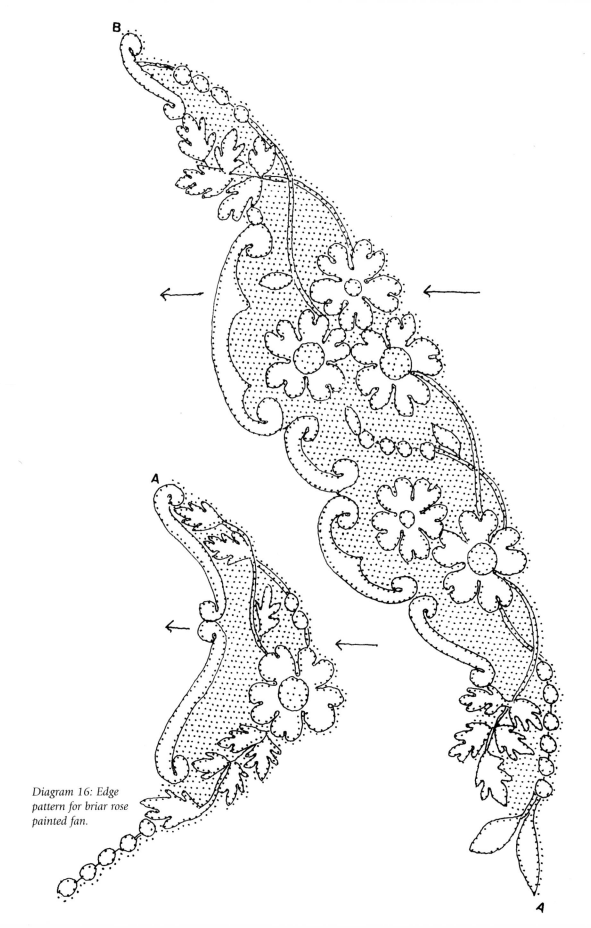

Diagram 16: Edge
pattern for briar rose
painted fan.

Diagram 17: Flower drawings to use for painted fans.

Figure 22 (above): Painted Ovals. This edge was shaped to fit round five painted ovals. I painted different flower sprays on to stiff silk using acrylic paint and worked Bucks lace, leaving oval spaces for the paintings. The edges were attached to the lace and the rest of the silk cut away. The design for the lace was inspired by the swags of flowers on the sticks.

Figure 19 (page 38): Foxgloves. This was a design from Designs for Modern Lace *by Johann Hrdlocka, 1902. I adapted it with my own interpretation in Bedfordshire lace.*

Figure 20 (page 38): Painted Roses. I painted a long spray of roses on to stiff silk and worked a Bedfordshire curved lace edge to fit at the outer edge and the lower edge. The sticks fanned out to a quarter-circle.

Figure 23 (right): This is a simple repeat pattern worked in rainbow colours with a silver gimp. Worked from diagram 18 a and b.

CHAPTER 2
USING COLOUR IN BOBBIN LACE

Using colour in bobbin lace can give a whole new concept of lace as a textile. Colour is employed widely in all forms of embroidery, weaving and knitting so it seems logical to use it in lacemaking with the enormous range of threads that are available. Introducing colour into needlelace is simple, as can be seen in Chapter 3.

Bobbin lace, however, creates a different problem. The passive threads that are in the lace weaving process have also to make the openwork background, so many of the techniques for a multi-thread one-colour lace have to be modified. The design and movement of the several colours has to be worked out carefully beforehand and the design coloured in on the paper pattern.

Using a coloured weaver in the solid areas and black, cream or white for the passives is the most satisfactory way. The coloured areas are worked in cloth stitch or half stitch and the use of fancy filling stitches confined to the background. Black passives give a more dramatic effect but it is important to use a very bright coloured thread as a weaver because it is toned down by the passives. Sometimes a shiny or

tinsel thread can be used to contrast with a duller thread background.

Work is always carried out on the wrong side so that the coloured thread can sometimes be carried over instead of cutting off.

Why put colour into bobbin lace at all? Its beauty lies in its fancy stitches, which create shadow and dimension without the use of colour. I would argue, however, that there is a place for both.

The correct choice of technique and colour scheme is all-important in making a piece of artistic merit. The use of colour makes lacemaking more exciting and stimulating and the more one does the more adventurous one becomes, as can be seen in Chapter 5.

Bobbin lacemaking is time-consuming and one has to be prepared to experiment before a final decision can be made on technique, colour, design and choice of thread.

Torchon is the easiest lace in which to use colour: its geometric formation gives one control of the coloured threads as can be seen from the patterns that follow.

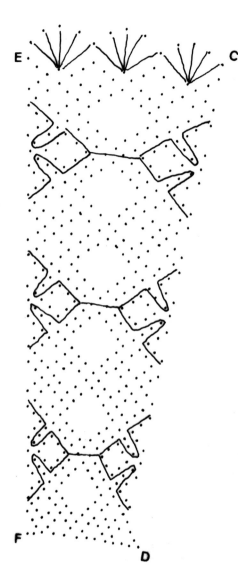

THE RAINBOW FAN

Materials: 68 pairs DMC 30 black, silver gimp, 1 pair each of orange, yellow, green, blue, indigo and violet, indicated O, Y, G, B, IN, V on diagram 18b. Use bright colours, Madeira rayon or stranded cotton.

- Make the pattern by matching CD to CD and repeating CDEF nine times with the large pattern ABCD reversed.
- The pattern is plotted on polar graph paper so that there are curved lines to the ground.
- Start at A with a trail from A to B, working in the direction of the arrows and adding pairs as required.
- The passives are black and the small diamonds are in half stitch. Work each large diamond in a different rainbow colour, with the shell edge in black. Work each large flower in cloth stitch in black with a silver gimp surround.
- The coloured weavers from the diamonds travel to the centre of the flower (an extra twist after working the stitch) and work a tally at the centre. They then travel back again to start the next diamonds.
- Continue to the end and finish off the threads in the final trail.

Diagram 18a and 18b (left and right): Pattern for Torchon rainbow fan.

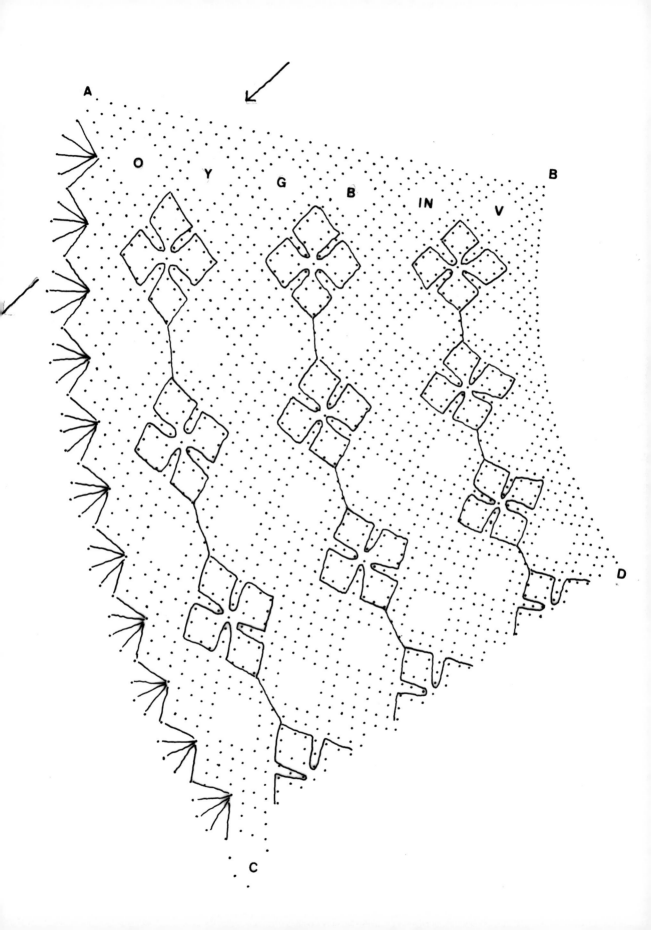

Figure 24: Coloured Blocks. This was worked in three shades of pink and three shades of green from diagram 19. It will fit doll-size sticks or can be enlarged to fit slightly larger sticks.

COLOURED BLOCKS
Materials: 26 pairs 80 Cotona black, 3 shades pink and 3 shades green.
Start at A and work in the direction of the arrows, making cloth stitch diamonds with coloured weavers. Graduate the colours from light to dark. Each weaver follows through to the next diamond.

There is a small band of rose ground in between the green blocks and the pink ones and the edge is a Spanish fan worked in pink. This pattern fits the miniature fan sticks that are available and can be enlarged to fit other sticks.

Figure 25: Clematis. This was planned on polar graph paper, using Bucks ground in black with coloured rayon threads as weavers for the flowers and leaves. The rayon threads are bolder in colour than the cotton ones and give a more dramatic effect with black. The idea came from a birthday card and the pattern appeared in Lace in Colour, *published by BT Batsford in 1990.*

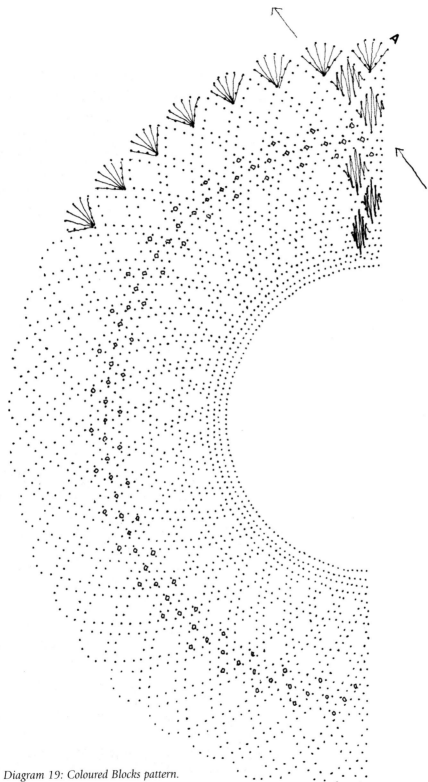

Diagram 19: Coloured Blocks pattern.

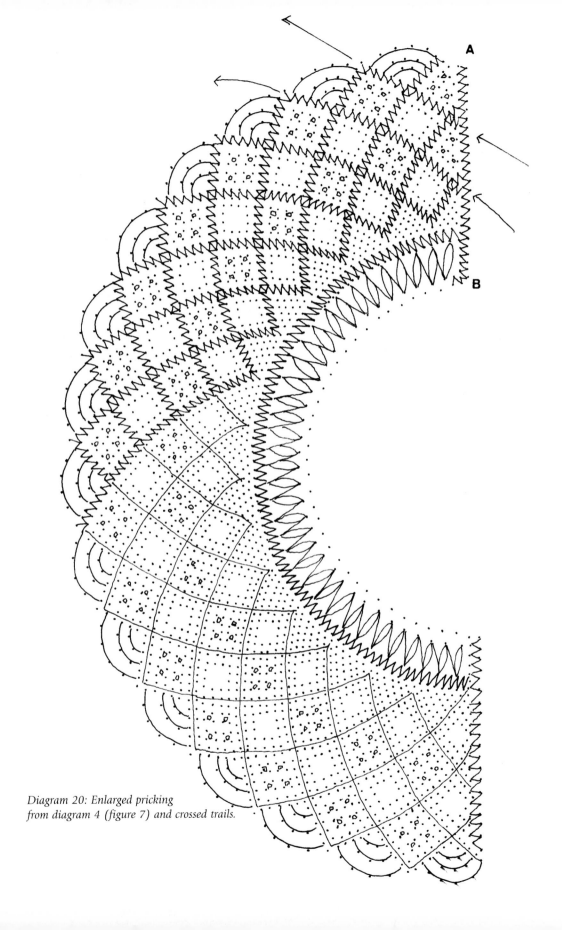

*Diagram 20: Enlarged pricking
from diagram 4 (figure 7) and crossed trails.*

Figure 26: Silver Gilt fan. I used the same idea as in the Clematis fan with different flowers and introduced a double ground in gold and black at the base to complement the silver gilt sticks.

CROSSED TRAILS

Materials: 32 pairs black Cotona 80, 7 pairs green and 2 pairs pink.

This pattern is a repeat of diagram 4, figure 7, enlarged 140 per cent and worked in black with bright tinsel colours (see diagram 20).

Start at A and work a cloth stitch trail from A to B and working the ground following the directional arrows. Work the diamond blocks with coloured weavers and use coloured weavers for the trails which meet and cross. Take the weaver from the diamonds across the trail to continue and alternate rose ground with the cloth stitch blocks.

Make the upper edge with plaits and picots in black and the lower edge in plaits and woven leaves from one lower trail to the next. Finish in a cloth stitch trail and cut off the threads as they accumulate.

Floral Bucks with colour introduced is more diffi-cult because of the curved shapes, but the two fol-lowing patterns will give some idea of what can be achieved.

*Figure 27: Poppies worked from diagram 21 and
mounted on plain bone sticks.*

POPPIES

Materials: 80 pairs 60 DMC, 5pairs red Madeira 50
and 4 pairs green Madeira 50.

Make the pattern by reversing and matching the
centre EF. The pattern has been plotted on hexagon
format and the change of direction will occur at CD.
Point ground, honeycomb and mayflower are the
fillings and, being worked in black, all the solid areas
are worked in half stitch with coloured weavers used
for poppy petals, stalks and leaves.

Begin at A and follow the arrows for direction; all
pairs are on by B. Introduce a green weaver for the
stalk and another where it meets the leaf. Work leaf
with a surround of black gimp in two halves,
dropping pairs out for the other half. Work the bud
in red and continue to the flower. Work each petal
with a new red weaver but carry them over if you can,
surrounding each in a black gimp. Tie out at the end
of the coloured area and continue the pattern in
black. At CD note the change of direction indicated
by the arrow at C. Stamens and centre are
embroidered on afterwards with bullion knots.

This pattern can be worked in a single colour
if desired.

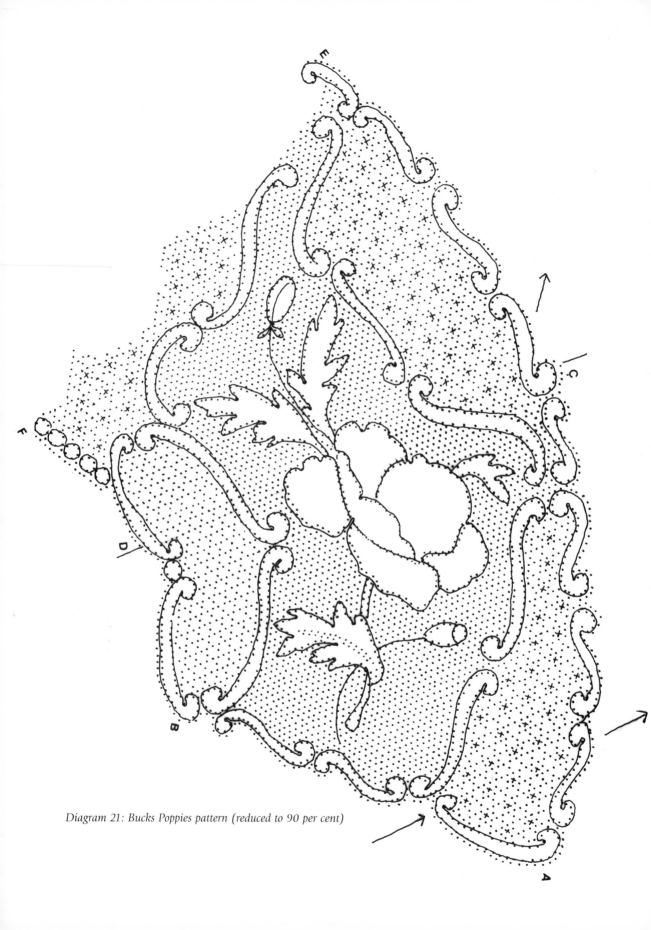

Diagram 21: Bucks Poppies pattern (reduced to 90 per cent)

Diagram 22: Christmas Bells pattern.

*Figure 28: Christmas Bells. This was made for a
Christmas card. Work from diagram 22.*

CHRISTMAS BELLS

Materials: 90 pairs 60 DMC black, 5 pairs gold
Madeira, 3 pairs red Madeira and 2 pairs green.
Several black gimp perlé 12 and red perlé 8.

This is a more difficult pattern as it uses many
colours and there is much more definition. It is a
hexagon format and the change in direction occurs
at DE centre.

To make the pattern reverse at DE, matching the
design. Beginning at A, work the half stitch trail to
B, adding pairs to plait and picot to the second trail.
Leave pairs out for the gimped honeycomb rings
and work these down to C while adding pairs on
this edge to work the point ground in the direction
of the arrows. Use red weavers for the poinsettia
petals and a gold weaver for the centres. Tie these off

when no longer needed. Make the berries with
honeycomb rings and use gimp 'fingers' for leaves in
black. Work each bell centre in black half stitch over
a gold leaf tally and work the outside of the bell
with a gold weaver. Work the holly leaves in two
parts with bright green weavers meeting each time at
the centre vein. Make picots on the holly leaf points.
Use red gimp to surround the holly berries.

The pattern changes direction at DE for the other side, but
it is better to include the centre bell F and the
centre poinsettia petal G in the second side for
continuity. Pairs will accumulate in the holly leaf at
H; remove some of them and add them again in the
next section when needed. The green weavers carry
on through. All threads can be cut off as they
accumulate at the end.

Figure 29: Miniature fans. Work from diagram 23.

MINIATURE FAN

Materials: 26 pairs 80 Cotona, 3 pairs gimp perlé 12.
This fan can be used as a brooch or on sticks (made with thin slivers of wood) for a doll. Work BCHK for a fan on sticks or the whole pattern with mock worked sticks for mounting in a brooch or picture.
Start at A with two pairs and three pairs on B as directed. Weave one pair of gimp through from B and leave to the left. Add pairs as indicated on the inside of the trail from B to C, and also on the outer edge where shown. Twist these four times and weave them through the gimp before use. Other pinholes on the outer edge are worked as picots.

Add one pair gimp at D as a stalk and carry it through the net to surround the flower. Add another pair of gimp for the lower edge honeycomb rings. Finish the tallies (12 weavers for each) before starting the flower. Complete the first flower using coloured weavers for the petals and turn the pillow to change direction for the next half. Continue to the end as indicated, taking out pairs as they accumulate.

When making the fan with mock sticks, take plaits from the lower edge backwards and forwards to the central point L. The flowers can be worked as honeycomb rings if working in a single colour.

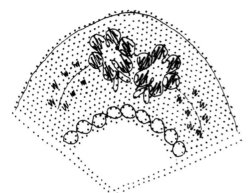

Diagram 23: Miniature fan pattern (reduced to 90 per cent).

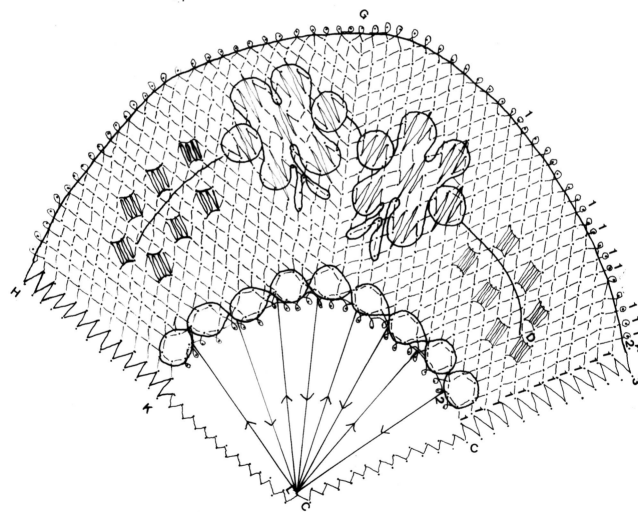

THE SEASONS

This project (see pages 58–9), spanning a few years, tries to capture the same scene at different times of the year. I set trees in the foreground with a stream behind, indicating distance and forming the backdrop.

WINTER

This was the first piece, and I wanted to give the impression of the starkness of trees against snow and to be able to use the numerous filling stitches that are the beauty of bobbin lace. I chose an Art Deco set of fan sticks, because with their elliptical shape they give a lot more scope for the centre of the design and require fewer bobbins.

I had to change my usual bobbin techniques to work the design: no longer was a one-piece lace possible as I wanted to create depth, with some parts lying on top of the background and yet joined to it. Honiton techniques were worked alongside Torchon, Bucks and Beds to create the idea.

To work in this way one has to think and work in reverse. In other words, the parts that are in the forefront have to be worked first, in this case the tree trunks, then the background worked on top, joining to them at intervals.

Working on the wrong side, one cannot see the effect until finished so some experience is necessary before attempting this method. This gives one however, the opportunity to use different colours for sky, fields, water and so forth.

I have used this method many times and have always found it successful.

The angle of the ground is is no longer important as it is worked in strips across the fan and can be plotted on normal 90 graph paper of appropriate size.

Once the scene was finished, it needed an animal of some sort. I chose a deer which was worked in one piece using Honiton techniques without the numerous 'sewings' and in several shades of fawn and brown. This fan was very pleasing so I began to think about spring.

SPRING

This was worked in the same way as the winter fan, but with a different colour scheme.

I wanted to capture the mistiness of early morning, with bluebells and trees just beginning to leaf. I have found that 8-thread Armure (a stitch found in the *Book of Lace Stitches* by Bridget Cook and Geraldine Stott) works well when mixed colours for sky or sea are required. The colours blend without forming lines or blocks. The trees are a softer shade and the green has to have the freshness of spring. Colour choice was very important. In spring, new life is born so I have included a doe and her fawn.

SUMMER

This was less successful: in summer green dominates as all the trees are in full leaf, there are daisies in the grass and some rape-seed yellow but otherwise it seemed very dull. I finally chose insects, butterflies and dragonflies as my animal life, especially as the sticks I had were embellished with insects.

AUTUMN

This was again much more colourful, with reds, browns and yellows in predominance. This colour combination continued with the choice of a pheasant. The green of autumn has become toned with yellow and brown and the tree trunks begin to darken. I enjoyed working on this series as it was like painting with threads.

Figure 30 (above): Spring.   *Figure 31 (below): Winter.*

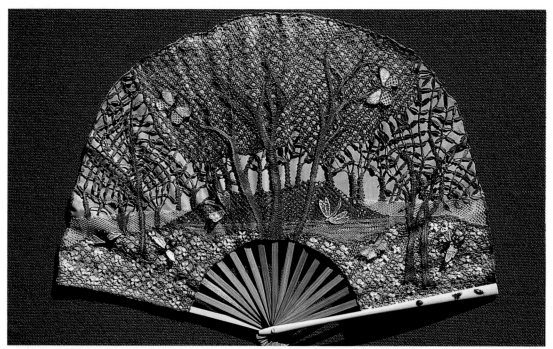

Figure 33 (below): Autumn.   *Figure 32 (above): Summer.*

CHAPTER 3
NEEDLELACE

If you have any interest in embroidery, needlelace is a comparatively easy skill and improves with practice.

When fully developed, there are very few limitations to design, unlike bobbin lace. A couched thread can be made to travel the same route as any drawn line and the shapes that are formed can be filled with dense or open stitches to create textures. The motifs can be joined by worked bars or by open needle-made net, and there is no difficulty in starting or ending threads. Needlelace can be as free as any other form of free-style embroidery.

Its technique has changed little since the 17th century when it was worked in white or ecru but whereas then certain stitches were copyright to different lace-making areas in Europe, we can use all of them for whatever design we choose.

THE BASIC STEPS

Diagram 24: Couching.

The stitch used is usually referred to as buttonhole stitch but it is not the same as the buttonhole in embroidery, which has a twist; it resembles loop or blanket stitch.

1. Trace the design on to firm tracing paper.
2. Cover with plastic film (book covering).
3. Tack firmly to a double piece of fabric (sheeting).
4. Couch a double thread with a finer thread (one that will break easily) round the design, through paper and the double fabric. The stitches should be 2 mm apart. Secure the couching thread at the back with a few stitches and start a new one with a knot as these threads are all removed at the end. This forms the framework on which the lace is worked.
5. Work filling stitches in the open areas, attaching and finishing off this thread by whipping it to the foundation. These stitches do not go through the paper and fabric but are worked on the surface. Always make sure you have enough thread to finish a row of stitches as it is difficult to finish off a thread in the middle.
6. Make worked bars if indicated.
7. Lay two threads along the same line as the original couching and buttonhole closely over them. This forms the hard raised outline so any number of threads can be used depending on the desired effect.
8. Remove the tacking and pull the two pieces of fabric apart, cutting the couch threads if necessary. If a very fine thread has been used, these threads break easily.
9. Remove the lace from the paper and pick out the remaining couch threads.

FILLING STITCHES

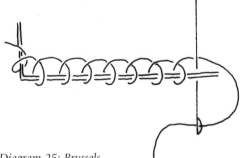

Diagram 25: Brussels.

BRUSSELS STITCH

Introduce a thread by whipping a few stitches to the outline. With the needle away from you, work an even row of buttonhole stitches through the couched threads so that the stitches lie on the surface. At the end of the row, take the thread under and over the couched threads and turn the work.

Work the next row of stitches from left to right with the needle towards you, into each loop of the previous row. Continue until the space is filled, then whip the filling to the upper couched threads. Always make sure you have enough thread to finish the row and finish and start each new thread by whipping it on to the couched threads.

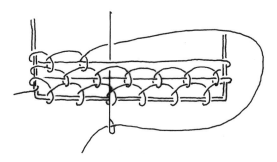

Diagram 26: Corded Brussels.

CORDED BRUSSELS STITCH
Introduce the thread as before by whipping to the foundation and work a row of Brussels stitch. When you reach the right-hand side, take the thread under and over the edge and straight back to the left-hand side. Take the thread under and over the edge and repeat the first row through the loop and including the laid thread.

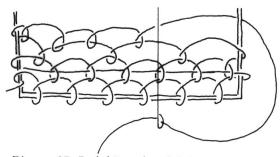

Diagram 27: Corded Brussels with holes

A ROW OF HOLES
This can be used to break up the solid corded Brussels to form veins or stripes.

After several rows of corded Brussels, instead of taking the thread across, turn the work and, with the needle towards you, work a row of Brussels stitch in alternate stitches. On the return row work two stitches in each large loop, then carry on with corded Brussels until the next row of holes is required. If used as a filling this worked at regular two-row intervals makes a striped filling.

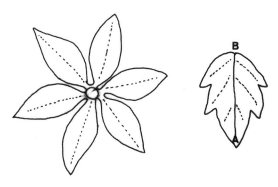

Diagram 28: Poinsettia flower and leaf pattern.

POINSETTIAS
These are a set of leaves and flowers that can be used as decoration; I have used them on a plain background of bobbin lace as a fan.

THE LEAVES
Materials: Green Madeira 30, DMC 30, 1strand of stranded cotton or silk.
Trace the pattern, mark in the dotted lines and cover with plastic film.
    Tack to a double piece of fabric.
    Couch a double green thread round the design starting at A on the vein and continuing round to B.
Work corded Brussels with one thread of the couched pair in rows from B following the direction of the dotted line. Work a row of holes on the dotted line to form a vein and then resume the corded Brussels to the next vein.
    Turn at the top of the leaf and continue to the top vein with a row of holes on the top dotted line on the other side of the leaf. Finish at B and fasten off.

FIgure 34: Poinsettias. Three-dimensional poinsettias
on a Torchon background made as a Christmas card.

EDGE STITCHING

Lay two threads round the design again, starting at the top of the centre vein and following the same route as the original couching. Buttonhole closely over these and the couched outline to form a neat edge. Make 11 leaves.

THE FLOWERS

Materials: Use the same size thread but in red.

Trace the pattern, mark in the dotted lines and cover with plastic film. Couch a double red thread round the flower, starting in the centre. Use one thread of the couched pair to work the filling. Work in the direction of the dotted line and make a row of holes on this line when reached. Continue round the flower and fasten off. Make five flowers.

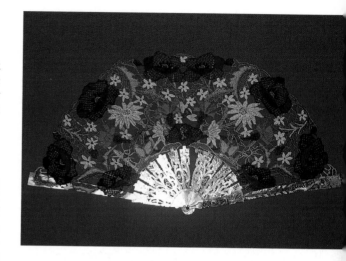

Figure 36 (above): Poppies. This was worked in needlelace using many different colours.

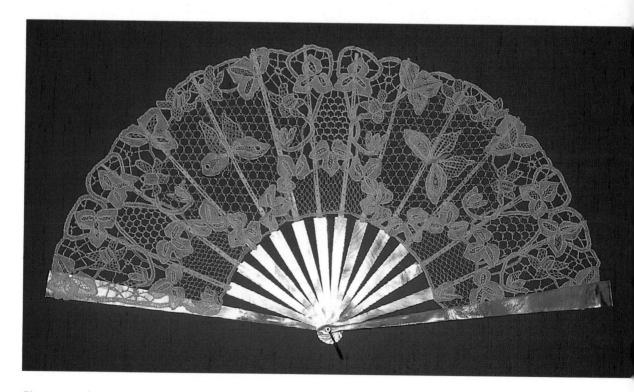

Figure 35: White needlelace. This was the same design as featured in diagram 41, but enlarged and worked in needlelace. This was the first fan I made in needlelace and it acted as a practice piece.

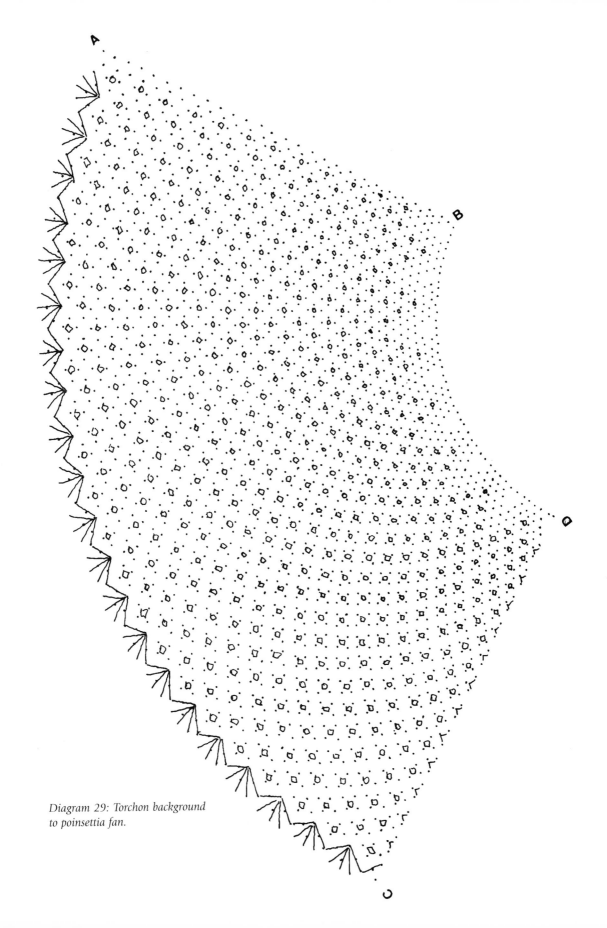

*Diagram 29: Torchon background
to poinsettia fan.*

WIRING

The petals can be left unwired, in which case work the edge stitching as for the leaves, but to give dimension to them wire must be added at this stage.

Fuse wire is suitable for most small flowers but thicker wire is necessary for heavier flowers.

Whip the wire to the outer edge and cut off. Proceed with the edge stitching as before in the leaves but work the close buttonhole over threads, wire and couched threads.

THE BOBBIN BACKGROUND

To make the poinsettia fan, a background is needed and although the flowers could be sewn on to fabric or net, it is infinitely better to put them on a bobbin-lace base.

Reverse the pattern at CD and start at A with a trail to B, adding pairs as needed. Work rose ground in the direction of the arrows with small cloth stitch triangles at the base and a simple shell fan at the top.

Apply the leaves and attach the flowers by their centres using small gold beads.

WORKED BARS

These are marked on a pattern as lines joining one motif to another and are worked before the edge stitching.

Attach a thread by whipping to the foundation, and take it across the space three times and buttonhole over them.

When a series of bars are to be worked, finish one and whip the thread to the next and continue.

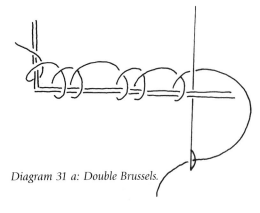

Diagram 31 a: Double Brussels.

DOUBLE BRUSSELS STITCH

Work a series of stitches in pairs, each followed by a two-stitch space, with the needle away from you. At the end of the row, take the thread under the edge and turn your work. The next row is worked with the needle towards you, with two stitches in the space and missing the two stitches of the previous row. Continue in this way to form a brick pattern.

This method can use various combinations of worked stitches and spaces to form different patterns.

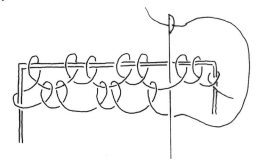

Diagram 31 b: Double Brussels.

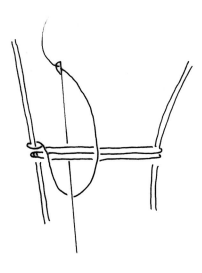

Diagram 30: Buttonhole bars.

Figure 37: Roses. This was the same pattern as for the Bedfordshire bobbin lace fan in Figure 17. The carved sticks required a heavier lace so I worked it in needlelace with beads in the flower centres and extra petals. The difference between bobbin lace and needlelace is apparent in the contrast of texture. It worked well with antique carved sticks. Bobbin lace would have been too delicate.

Figure 38: Dragons. The stylised needlelace dragons were applied on to a simple bobbin-lace background and were made to match a parasol that I had made earlier. I had acquired some sandalwood sticks which were decorated with spangles and had a narrow fan leaf area that suited my dragon idea. On the parasol the dragons are round the edge, so they had to be adapted for the fan. Simple corded Brussels with holes was used, worked in cream with edges in gold and mounted on a Torchon bobbin-lace background.

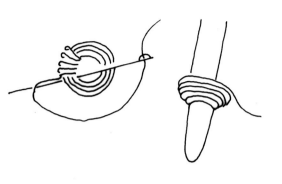

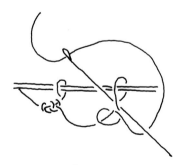

Diagram 34: Pea stitch.

Diagram 32: Couronnes.

COURONNES

These are used frequently as decoration and make excellent 'nests' in which to add beads or gems.

Thread a needle with a long length of thread and wrap the end several times round the tip of a fine knitting needle. Make two buttonhole stitches round the threads and gently take the ring off the knitting needle. Buttonhole completely round the ring and leave the thread for sewing into the desired place.

PEA STITCH

Work the first row in Brussels stitch from left to right with the needle away from you. Turn and, with the needle towards you, work two stitches, miss two stitches. Turn and work three stitches into the large loop and one stitch into the small loop.

Repeat the second row making sure that the two worked stitches come in the centre of the previous large loop and the two missed stitches are over the small loop.

Continue these two rows until the space is filled.

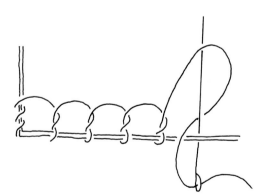

Diagram 33: Twisted Brussels stitch.

TWISTED BRUSSELS STITCH

Work from left to right and turn the work after each row. Form the twist by putting the thread from the needle under the needle, thus forming a twist. This is akin to the true buttonhole stitch in embroidery.

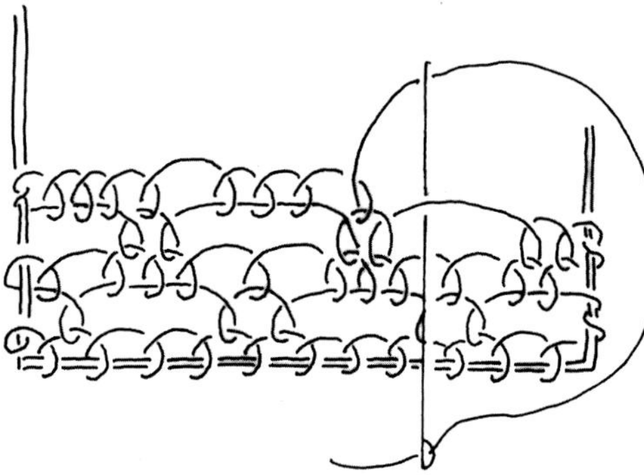

Diagram 35: Point de Venise.

POINT DE VENISE

This is a very useful stitch that will give a picot finish to a plain buttonholed edge.

Attach a thread to the edging and make a buttonhole stitch into the edge to the right. Work three buttonhole stitches into this loop and then repeat the process.

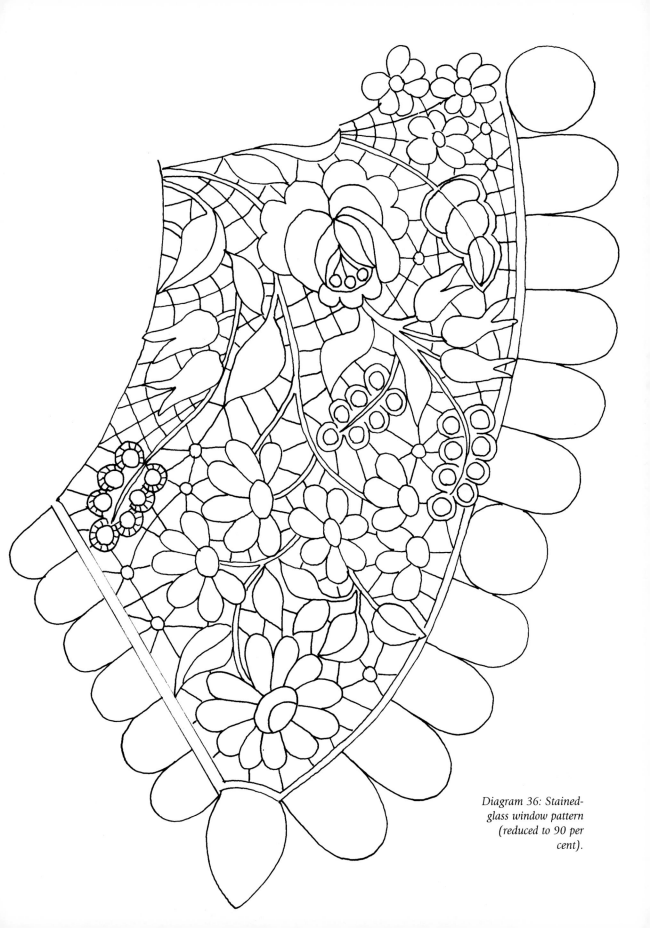

Diagram 36: Stained-glass window pattern (reduced to 90 per cent).

*Figure 39: Stained-glass window fan worked from
diagram 36.*

STAINED-GLASS WINDOW FAN

This was worked as an experiment to see if outlining the whole fan in black would give the desired effect, and the result was very good.

The design came from a piece of Hungarian embroidery worked in satin stitch in bright colours.

I used 30 thread in black for the outline and the final edge stitching, with stranded cotton and silk for the colours.

Make the pattern by reversing it and adjusting the centre flowers. Cover with plastic film and attach to fabric.

Use a double thread of black for the outline, couching with a fine thread. Work each area at a time rather than couching the whole design in one go, and when new threads are needed loop them in to a completed couched line and continue. This means that you can work some fillings and bars before completing the couching, and this makes it more interesting to complete.

The large leaves in the centre of the fan and the groups of red berries are made by first working a row of twisted buttonhole round the motif in black. The stitches in the filling are worked backwards and forwards to the loops of this rather than the couched edge. The berries are small circles, which are worked round and round in single Brussels stitch until the centre where they are fastened off.

The motifs look better if they are worked fairly solid in corded Brussels, with few open fillings.

Leave the outer edge until last when the whole fan is complete because at this stage you can decide on its colour scheme. This is worked in double Brussels round the curve and back to the straight in rows. There will be an opening slit in the centre. The circles are worked round and round, to finish in a centre hole. Make sure that you have a long enough thread to complete the rounds.

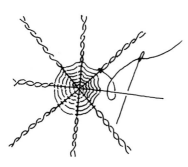

Diagram 37: Spider's web.

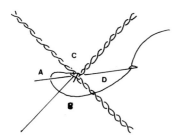

Diagram 38: Bud.

Figure 40: Golden wedding fan made to celebrate the author's golden wedding anniversary; see diagram 39.

SPIDER'S WEB

This is worked on laid threads that meet at the centre, forming spokes. The laid thread is whipped to form a twist instead of being buttonholed. Before the last spoke is worked make a continuous web by taking the needle under and back over each spoke. When sufficient rows have been worked, make a buttonhole stitch to secure and continue whipping the final spoke.

BUD

This gives a raised knot at the crossing of two threads.

Whip the three threads to the X and work one buttonhole stitch through the X towards A, turn, and work two buttonhole stitches towards B. Turn, and work three buttonhole stitches towards C, turn and work a final buttonhole stitch towards D, pulling it tight to bunch the stitches. Continue to whip the fourth thread of the crossing.

Diagram 39: Golden wedding fan pattern.

GOLDEN WEDDING FAN

This fan was designed to celebrate my golden wedding and was worked in cream and gold with amber jewels. It could be made for a silver wedding in white and silver with diamond jewels or for any other one with ruby jewels, emeralds, etc. Materials: DMC 30 in cream, Madeira gold 40, millinery wire and thin wire, 13 jewels or beads.

Reverse the pattern and cover with plastic film; tack to double fabric.

Couch a double cream thread round the whole design, and with the thin thread make small cross stitches on the ground lines where the threads meet, also on the picots of the outer edge. Complete all the fillings as indicated, A in pea stitch, B in double Brussels and the rest in corded Brussels.

THE BACKGROUND

Attach a thread to the outline and take the thread through the crosses to the opposite side in a straight line; whip the thread back to the starting point again through the crosses (this forms a twist on the thread).Repeat until there are some crossings of threads. The initial thread can be whipped along the outline until another position is reached. Where two threads meet make a bud and where eight threads meet work a spider's web.

When the background is complete, work the edge stitching with two threads of cream laid on the cream parts and two threads of gold on the gold parts. Buttonhole closely over these threads, make couronnes in the flower centres.

Whip thin wire to the outline of the external sprays and buttonhole closely over wire and laid threads. Whip millinery wire to the outer shape and buttonhole over it and the laid threads. Work the outer loop and picot edge as shown in diagram 40.

Make four extra flowers and the petals for the central flower. Work these in corded Brussels in the direction of the dotted line, making a row of holes on these lines. Edge stitch these and apply them to the main fan. The couronnes in the flower centres form 'nests' in which to insert beads or jewels.

Mount on a turned stick with PVA. glue.

OUTER PICOT EDGE

Work this after buttonholing the edge.

Attach a thread to a buttonhole stitch at A and take it to the position of the next loop to be made at B. Take it backwards and forwards twice (4 threads) ending at A. Work close buttonhole over these threads to B.

Repeat B to C as from A to B, but buttonhole only halfway to D. At this point take the thread back to the centre of the first loop at E, backwards and forwards ending at E (3 threads).

Buttonhole to the centre above the X to make the picot. Take the thread through the cross and back to the loop, ending at the X. Buttonhole from X to loop and continue buttonholing to D. Finish the loop from D to C. Continue until all the edge is complete.

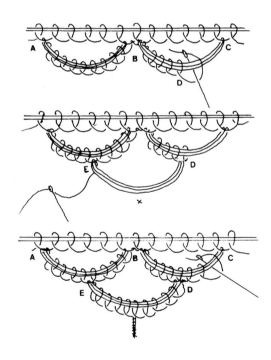

Diagram 40: Golden wedding outer looped edge pattern.

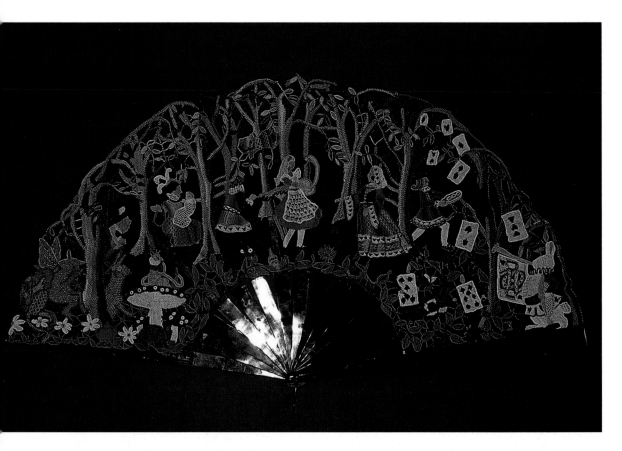

Figure 41 (above): Alice in Wonderland. Needlelace figures mounted on net, Griffin and Mock Turtle, Mad Hatter, March Hare, Dormouse, Duchess with the baby turning into a pig, the King of Hearts with the Cheshire Cat, Alice playing croquet with a flamingo and a hedgehog, the Queen of Hearts, the Knave with the tarts, painting the roses red, the White Rabbit, Caterpillar on the toadstool and the cards tumbling down. All colours are taken from playing cards. All are set in a woodland scene.

Figure 42 (top right): Alice Through the Looking Glass. This was made as a companion to Alice in Wonderland, and worked in needlelace and mounted on net, with antique sticks. Alice and the White and Red Queens, Tweedledum and Tweedledee, the Red and White Knights, the Jaberwock, the talking flowers and the Walrus and the Carpenter.

Figure 43 (bottom right): Chrysanthemums. These were worked in needlelace on a bobbin-lace background. The idea was taken from a book on Chinese theatrical decoration.

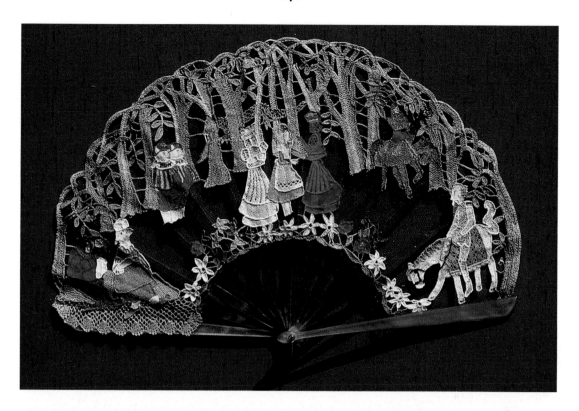

CHAPTER 4
EMBROIDERED LACES

Both Carrickmacross and Limerick are embroidered laces and are worked on machine-made net. They are used together in many cases.

CARRICKMACROSS

This is appliquéd fabric on net and it is important to use a delicate transparent material to give the required lacy appearance. Use cotton net with cotton organdie, silk tulle with silk organza or nylon net with any man-made organzas.

Use Madeira 30 or equivalent for the laid thread and 80 for the couching.

Prewash cotton net and organdie to shrink them.

BASIC STEPS

1. Trace the pattern using a dark line that will show through net and fabric.
2. Cover with plastic film.
3. Place the net on top of the design, stretching it slightly and tack through the paper.
4. Place the fabric on top of the net and tack again, make a few tacking stitches in between the pattern to hold it firmly.
5. Take enough thicker thread to go round the design in a continuous line and couch this with the thinner thread. Make stitches only through the net and fabric 1mm apart and not through the paper. The plastic film covering is there to help the needle slide along the surface. At flower indentation or at a dead-end, couch threads up and back. Start and finish the couching threads by backstitching.
6. Make traditional Carrickmacross looped edging on the top edge.
7. When finished, remove all tacking stitches and lift the lace from the pattern.
8. Cut away the fabric from the background of the design, leaving the net exposed. Take great care as one careless snip can ruin the work. In confined spaces such as flower centres, lift the organdie between the fingers and make a small snip first.
9. Select the areas for filling with Limerick darning and work patterns from the diagrams.

CARRICKMACROSS FAN

This can be reduced or enlarged to fit the sticks.

Trace the pattern and its reverse with a strong dark line and cover with plastic film. You may find this easier to handle while working by tacking it to a piece of material.

Follow the basic steps outlined, and finish off the outer edge with Carrickmacross loops. Fill all areas marked A with Limerick fillings of your choice and work surface embroidery on the flower centres and butterfly wings. Cut out the centres of leaves.

CARRICKMACROSS LOOPS (POPS)

Couch another thread along the outline and make a large loop at the marked position, couch this with three stitches close together then gently pull the loop to the correct size.

Couch along to the next loop position and repeat.

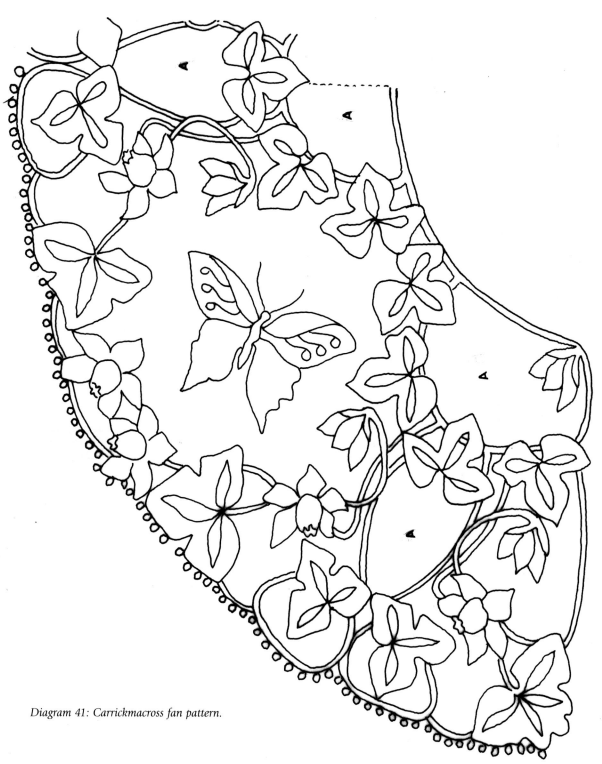

Diagram 41: Carrickmacross fan pattern.

Figure 44: Carrickmacross in traditional form. This is worked from diagram 41.

Figure 45: Red Dragon. Carrickmacross is traditionally worked in white, but I have experimented with colour, using coloured organdie or organza and also darning the net behind the motifs to form shadow work (see Colour in Lace, Batsford 1990). The dragon sticks were very large and needed a bold design. I used red organdie and applied it to black net with a laid gold thread. Further additions of gold kid and gold embroidery enhanced the overall effect.

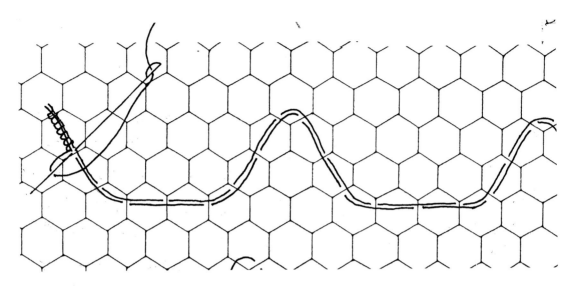

Diagram 42: Scalloped edge showing darning and buttonhole finish

LIMERICK

This is darning on net and there are many variations and combinations that can produce a wealth of attractive filling stitches.

I have given you a wide selection of my favourites and over several years have worked them into a sampler fan. Many will combine together to form yet other patterns.

Use a soft thread for the darning (stranded cotton), two threads for the outline and one thread for the fillings.

BASIC STEPS

1. Attach the net to an embroidery frame so that it lies with the grain (lines of net) in a north/south, east/west direction when under tension.
2. Trace the intended pattern and tack it to the underside of the net with the pen lines on the reverse side so that they do not touch the lace but are plainly visible.
3. Using two strands darn in and out of the net following the pattern lines from the drawing underneath. It is sometimes necessary to go over or under two to keep the continuity of the design. Use long lengths of thread although it is possible to bring another one in by running it

alongside the other for a short distance.
4. When all the outlining is complete, remove the pattern from the net but leave the net on the frame.
5. Make fillings in the solid design areas by attaching a thread to the outline and working diagonal darning, straight darning or zig-zag darning.
6. Work open filling stitches in the other areas.
7. Buttonhole stitch the outer areas and cut the net away from these.

LIMERICK SAMPLER FAN

This pattern can be reduced or enlarged to fit the sticks or be made into a round as a parasol. Repeat the design as many times as required, then follow the basic steps.

Work different fillings in areas A but work the same all-over pattern in B. I used honeycomb in silver. The solid areas are worked in variations of close darning with buttonhole stitch rings in the flower centres. Finish the top, bottom and side edges with close buttonhole stitch.

This fan design could also be worked in Carrickmacross with the addition of Limerick fillings.

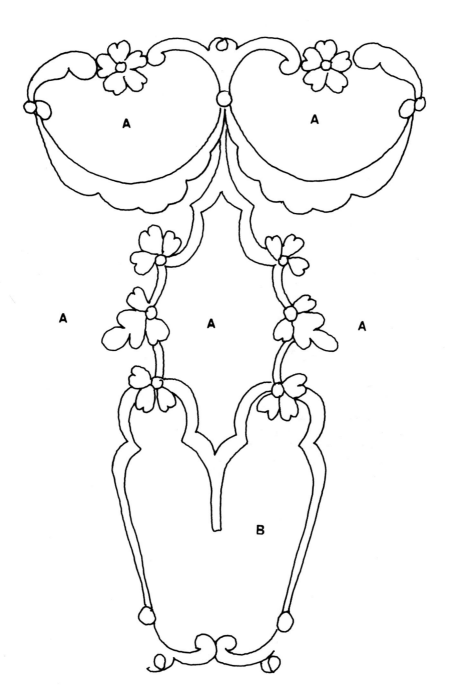

Diagram 43: Limerick Sampler fan pattern.

Figure 46: Limerick Sampler that was worked over several years. Each time I found a different filling in a piece of antique lace, I made a diagram and worked it on my sampler. In the 1850s, the Limerick workers would have made a sampler first. This would be part of their learning but also useful for later work. When a new commission was set, the sampler would be put underneath the design and the most suitable one selected. The sampler fan can be worked from diagram 43.

*Figure 47:Flower Fairies. The idea came from the
Flower Fairy book by Cicely May Barker, and the fan
was a Carrickmacross/Limerick experiment. I noticed
that when cutting the organdie away at the end, it
curled up forming a three dimensional effect. I tried it
on the briar rose petals and then worked Limerick
fillings in colour underneath. I added some shadow
embroidery and worked the fairy wings in silver.*

LIMERICK FILLINGS

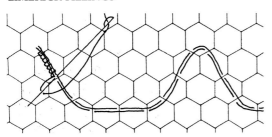

Diagram 43 (above): scalloped edge.
Darn two threads under and over the net following the required size of the scallop. Buttonhole closely so that the net can be cut away to it.

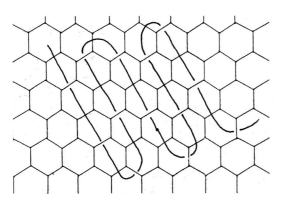

Diagram 44 (above): diagonal darning.
Simple under-and-over darning on the diagonal line of net. A double thread can be used for extra denseness.

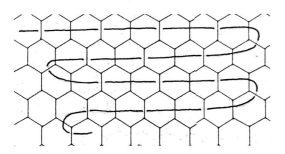

Diagram 45 (above): straight darning.
Simple under-and-over darning on the straight net. A double thread can be used.

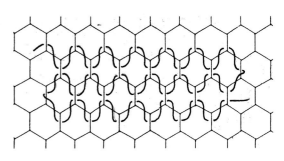

Diagram 46 (above): zig-zag darning.
This is worked on straight net, under and over one hole then to the row below.

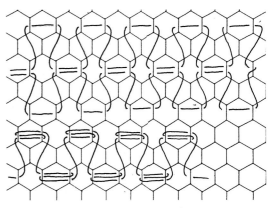

Diagram 47 (above): honeycomb.
This is a very good all-over pattern. Work under two bars, over two diagonal bars to the row below, under two bars and over two bars back to the row above. Repeat so that the next row is in reverse. This can be varied by working two or three stitches over the wide part as shown.

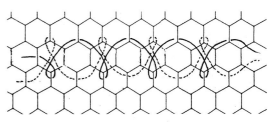

Diagram 48 (above): figure of eight.
This is worked in two movements. The first row is shown by the dark line and the second row, which overlaps, it is shown by the dotted line.

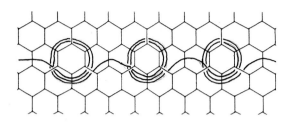

Diagram 49 (above): ring filling.
The thread travels three times round a net ring before moving to the next position. Keep loose, do not pull tight.

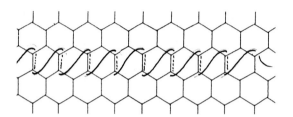

Diagram 50 (above): overcast stitches.
The thread passes over and under one row.

Cross stitch (not illustrated)
This is formed by working another set of overcasting in the opposite direction.

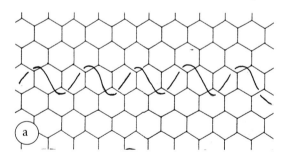

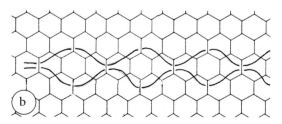

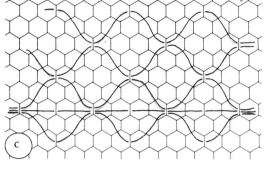

Diagram 51 a, b and c (above): wave stitches.
Various sizes can be created by using a different number of threads to go under and over. Straight darning can be incorporated for a different effect and they can be interspersed with ring filling.

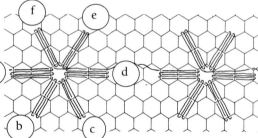

Diagram 52 (above): daisies.
These are more complicated than other stitches but, once mastered, make a very pretty filling.

Following the diagram, start at A and weave backwards and forwards over three bars (three times) to end in the centre. Repeat the weaving to B and back to the centre twice, then to C, to D, to E and to F. At the centre weave the thread back to D and work over and under to the next daisy position. Repeat.

*Figure 48: Foxgloves and dandelions. I have tried
many times to capture the gossamer seeds of the
dandelion in lace techniques, but they did not work
successfully until I discovered Limerick. Working large
daisies as in diagram 52 made excellent seeds and
they could be scattered at random. I used my sampler
to select fillings for the foxgloves. The sticks are gilded
mother-of-pearl.*

*Figure 49: The willow patterns. This is made in
needlelace on net; the sea was worked in Limerick
honeycomb filling in silver and I have included the
figures hurrying to the boat on the sea, with the island
in the distance.*

CHAPTER 5
COMBINING LACE TECHNIQUES

I have found that all the various methods of making lace work well together in one piece, the attributes of each contributing to the design.

Bobbin lace produces a soft lace and is good for textured backgrounds with the variety of its stitches. Needlelace is bold, easy to work in colour and can also take surface embroidery and beads without distortion of shape.

If needlelace pieces are applied to machine net, texture can be given to the net with Limerick fillings.

THE MASK

Materials: Sylko perlé 12 in white and black for the needlelace, with red, yellow and green Madeira 40 for the ribbons. Madeira 30 in white and black for the bobbin lace.

This is an example of needlelace with bobbin lace worked in as a background.

Reverse the pattern from AB, trace and cover with plastic film. Follow the basic steps for needlelace. Couch white thread in the black parts, black thread in the white parts and red, yellow and green on the ribbons.

Work corded Brussels starting on the line AB, one side in white and the other side in black, leaving a hole for the eye. Work pea stitch in C. At the end, edge stitch the black parts in white and the white parts in black, use self colour for the ribbons and gold round the tears and eyebrows.

Attach the pattern to a lace pillow and when the needlelace is completed, remove it from the pattern and pin it down firmly on its wrong side on the pattern.

Begin rose ground at D, adding pairs as required by hooking them into the ribbon edges with a very fine crochet hook. These threads are hooked in and passed over each ribbon, hooked in the opposite side and the ground resumed. All threads tie off in the main mask at the end. Work the other side.

Alternatively the mask (without the bobbin net) can be applied to machine net or with millinery wire incorporated into the edge stitching, applied to a turned stick as in the wedding fan.

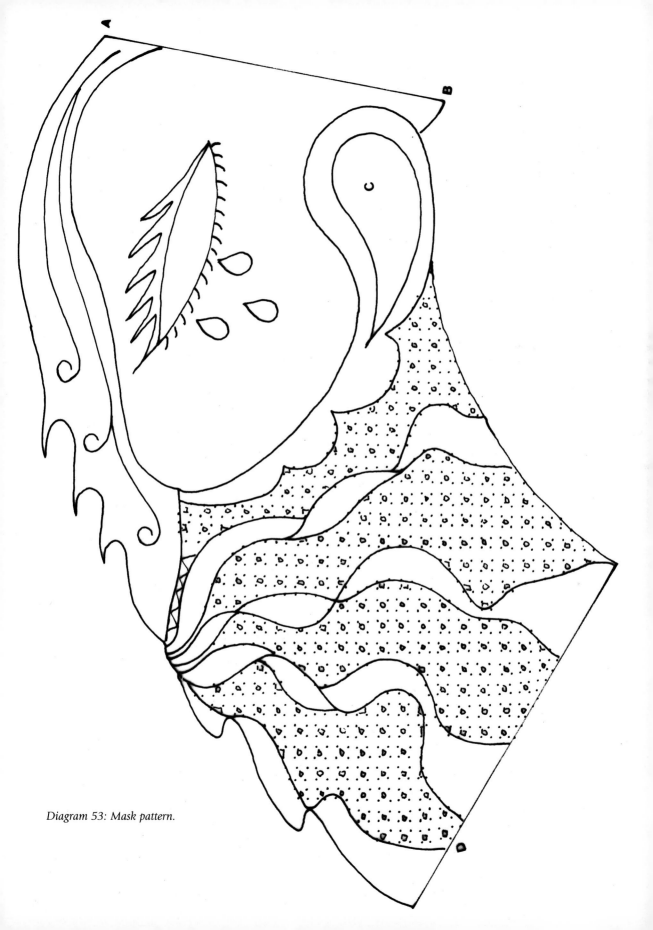

Diagram 53: Mask pattern.

*Figure 50: The Mask. This was made for a medieval
banquet and took three weeks to make. See diagram 53.*

*Figure 51: Stylised Flower. This combination of
techniques started with the purchase of some attractive
purple/pink thread. I decided on Art Deco elliptical
sticks so that I could have a large central flower motif.
The effect of dimension was created by the use of
stitches and colour; the flower and leaves were worked
in needlelace. The leaf shapes were from a Marenta
plant. The outer and lower edges were worked in
Bedfordshire bobbin lace with Torchon in a metallic
thread for the centre panel.*

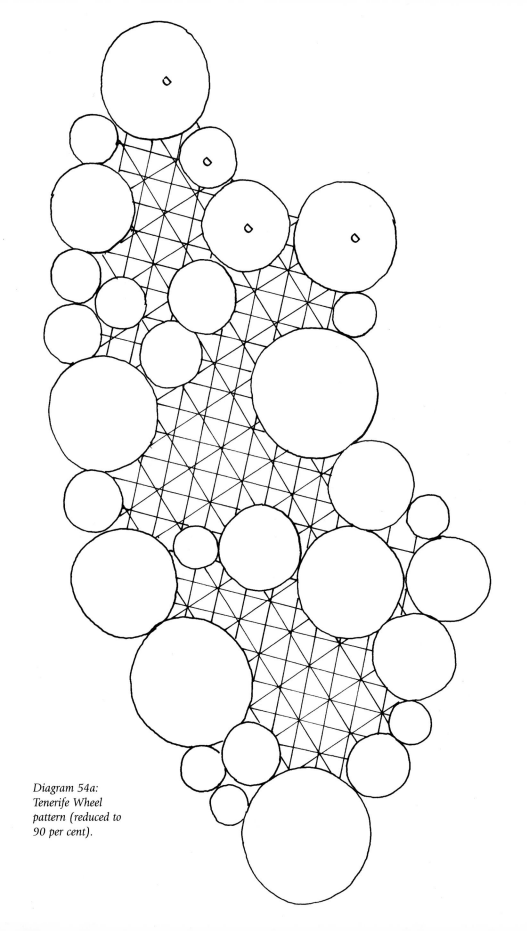

Diagram 54a:
Tenerife Wheel
pattern (reduced to
90 per cent).

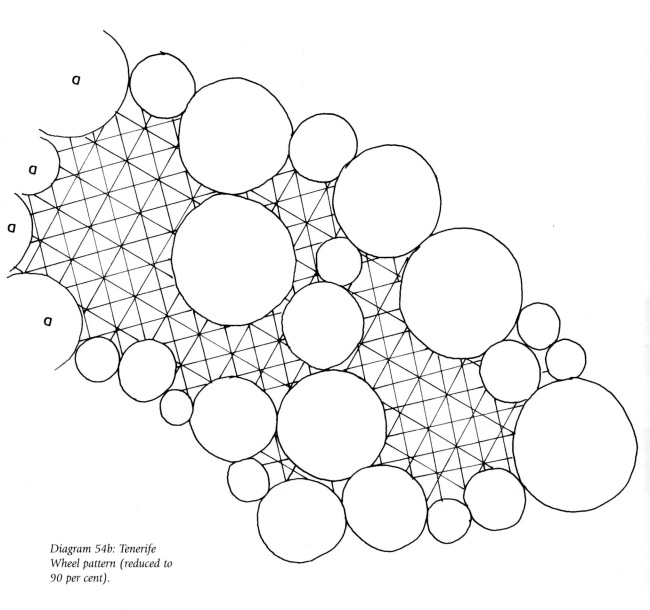

Diagram 54b: Tenerife
Wheel pattern (reduced to
90 per cent).

TENERIFE WITH NEEDLELACE

I have included the pattern of the Tenerife fan without the instructions for making Tenerife lace because the design of circles lends itself to interpretations in needlelace and also bobbin lace. I made only six Tenerife circles; the rest were all made in needlelace in various formations.

The ground was a Tenerife one but works equally well with the ground used in the Golden Wedding fan: buds where two threads cross and spider's webs where eight threads cross. Remember to make cross stitches in a thin thread

prior to working.

There are many patterns for rings in Buckinghamshire and Bedfordshire lace that could be used for this design, either applied to machine net or on a bobbin-lace ground.

To make the pattern, trace off the two parts, matching them at the centre.

Rings can be worked separately in bobbin lace or needlelace, then tacked firmly on to the pattern for the background to be worked.

This is the last of the patterns and is intended for you to interpret as you wish.

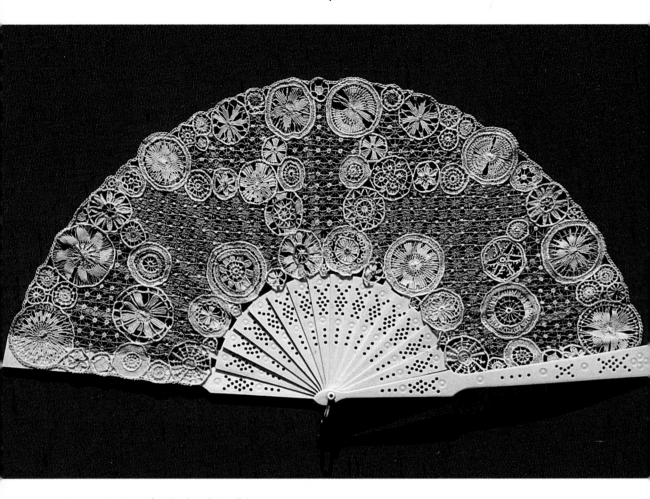

Figure: 52: Tenerife Wheel and Needlelace.

Figure 53: A close-up of the motifs and the ground of Tenerife Wheel and Needlelace.

MOUNTING AND FOLDING

I have never found an antique lace fan that has been sewn to the sticks; they were always stuck even though the sticks are often pierced with holes that could indicate stitches. The lace is sometimes held by stitches at top and bottom because, with constant folding and unfolding, these are the weakest points. The glue that was used was very light but firm and only when amateurs did repairs was the thick glue (secotine) used and this discoloured with age.

I use PVA and find it works well, dries clear and does not discolour but I have an unusual method of using it (see below).

Sometimes the lace needs a backing of material to show it off well, as the sticks detract from the design. Use a lightweight fabric and sew the lace on to it round the edge with small stitches. Paint Fray-check on the edge of the material on the sewing line and cut away the fabric to this. Follow the steps below to attach to sticks.

MOUNTING
Work on an ironing board.

1. Spread the sticks out evenly to the size of your lace.
2. Paint the inner sticks with glue and leave to nearly dry (five minutes). Do not paint the guard sticks yet. Pin the sticks to the ironing board.
3. Place the lace on top of the sticks, including the guard sticks and adjust its position. This must be very accurate. (the lace will not stick yet).
4. Cover with a dry cloth and press the lace to the sticks with a medium-hot iron.
5. Paint the guard sticks with glue and leave for five minutes.
6. Make sure the inner sticks are attached and iron the lace to the guard sticks as in step 4.

You will find that the lace adheres rather than sticks firmly but in this way there is no glue on the lace. Sometimes one or two inner sticks do not stick properly the first time. Paint glue on to the stick again, leave and re-iron.

FOLDING
In the days when fans were professionally made, no one was expected to pleat a fan leaf by hand; a mould, which was cut into grooves that radiated from the centre, was used. The number of grooves depended on the number of sticks, usually about 20. The worker would gently push the leaf over the surface of the mould, aligning the motifs or paintings. Then it was pressed down into the mould with a special tool. The folded leaf was then attached to the sticks and a rivet inserted in the head.

Obviously, as amateurs, we cannot work in this way. In any case, lace fans folded in rigid pleats take on a concertina effect, which does not show the lace off to advantage. I fold mine softly stick by stick, taking care that they each align, and then enclose with an elastic band for a day. They then fold quite naturally each time, with no trace of crease when unfolded.

CHAPTER 6
INSPIRATIONAL FANS

his chapter contains the rest of my fans, to show the possibilities for design. I have been making lace fans for over 25 years and over this time they have gradually become more adventurous in design. Many are in scenic form and inspiration comes from holidays, paintings, events, poetry, ballet, anything that sets off the imagination. There is in reality no end to the ideas.

When I first began, the only lace fans that I saw were very traditional and usually in black, white or ecru. Sometimes the lace was mixed with painting but I never saw whole scenes in coloured lace.

I did, however, have a collection of antique painted and textile fans and observed that the design was often painted as a complete picture with a piece cut out to accommodate the sticks. They were always planned in a semi-circle and the design allowed for this. It was these fans, rather than the colourless lace ones, that attracted me.

The beauty of lace fans lies in the intricacy of their stitches, and light, shade and dimension can be created merely by the choice of stitch.

My first attempts were worked within traditional bobbin lace techniques and this enabled me to discover its potential for design.

Proportion and symmetry are necessary in both single-colour and multicoloured lace. In traditional lace the important feature is the choice of fancy stitch to create depth and flow of design but when several colours are used, the balance of colour has to be observed as well.

As I have pointed out in previous chapters, the difficulty with bobbin lace in colour is the complication of ground work in conjunction with the solid areas.

Needlelace opens up a whole new area for design: working what is drawn on paper is no problem.

Many of the fans in this section include a mixture of techniques, often bobbin lace and needlelace. Bobbin lace is a softer flat lace and therefore useful for backgrounds and images in the distance. Needlelace is bolder and suitable for colourful figures in the foreground as well as three-dimensional lace, which can be further decorated or padded (stumpwork).

The wide variety of stitches found in antique bobbin lace and in needlelace can all be used to their best advantage to create scenes. Open stitches for sky and sea, more solid ones for pavements, grass, snow and so forth.

Many people ask me how I begin designing. I usually have one idea in my mind, another that is drawn out ready to work and one being made in either bobbin lace or needlelace.

The idea starts as a small doodle, giving me some idea of content and balance of the design within a fan shape. The fact that one is designing within a set shape has certain limitations, which I find helpful.

The doodle has to include the outer and lower edges, and various possibilities can be tried. When a satisfactory doodle emerges, it is enlarged and parts coloured in. Fan sticks are then selected and the technique and threads decided. Now it can be further enlarged and details drawn to fit the sticks. If bobbin lace, then the grounds are filled in as explained in Chapter 1.

The final design is plotted on firm tracing paper to the size of the fan and if bobbin lace is to be used then it is pinned on to firm card on a pillow ready for working. For small fans I use a normal large pillow of straw or polystyrene but for large fans, I prefer large polystyrene blocks that fit on to a board with a ledge. The blocks are added as the work progresses.

Needlelace pieces can be worked separately and then attached to the bobbin background, or in some cases these can be pinned down on to the pillow and the background worked over the top.

Designs entirely in needlelace are drawn on to tracing paper and covered with plastic film. I always work these as one piece and not in individual pieces.

I have endeavoured to explain the inspiration for each fan design, and outlined the techniques employed.

Figure 54: Japanese Motifs. This was worked in cross stitch on fine silk canvas with Bucks bobbin lace worked as a surround. I used a fine silk thread and a honeycomb ground with tallies (Mayflower). The carved sticks were very delicate and because they were quite old were meant for a fan of only a quarter-circle. The lace needed to be very lightweight.

Figure 55: My Home in the Rhododendrons. I worked the house in cross stitch on silk canvas and surrounded it with rhododendron flowers worked in needlelace. Some of the flowers are made separately and wired to give dimension.

Figure 56: English Butterflies. Butterflies are depicted frequently in both bobbin lace and needlelace; their shape, patterning and veining offering great scope for the many filling stitches. They often appear on fans, along with dragonflies and moths. When planning a fan with coloured butterflies, I looked through many books. The number of different shapes, sizes and colours became too confusing so I decided to work just English butterflies on a background of honeysuckle. They were worked in needlelace exactly as they appear in nature, with the tracery of veins and the correct patterning and colouration of their wings.

There is a Brimstone, a Purple Emperor, a Milkweed, a Peacock, a Red Admiral and a Swallowtail. The latter was wired and perched in the centre of the fan. The completed needlelace was attached to silk tulle.

Figure 57 (right): The Swallowtail. I enlarged the swallowtail to fan size, worked in needlelace with added beads. The wings were wired with millinery wire and the butterfly attached to a turned ebony stick.

Figure 58: Multicoloured Butterfly. This was worked in bobbin lace in a large number of coloured threads, stranded cotton, silk and tinsel. It was an early experiment in the use of colour in bobbin lace, and it was making this fan that gave me an insight into the way that a weaver can change the colour of a whole area. The intermingling of the threads work in much the same way as paints. A dark pink weaver through yellow passives gives an orange colouration. I decided to use the 'hot side' of the colour spectrum from yellow to mauve, changing the weaver colour and passives gradually.

It took very few bobbins as it was worked in tape lace techniques with 'sewings' as in Honiton, and the filling stitches in the open areas added later.

The body was worked in textured black threads with added beads and then lightly stuffed before being attached to the sticks.

Figure 59: The Hummingbird Moth. This was a combination of Bucks bobbin lace, needlerun (Limerick) and needlelace techniques. The design was inspired by a real moth that I photographed; it had very interesting colouration and patterning. The lower wings were worked in tape/Honiton with 'sewings' in alternating half and whole stitch. The upper wings were Bucks ground in gold, darned in a zig-zag pattern as in Limerick, and the body was worked in needlelace in chenille and mohair. It was mounted on a turned stick with a cross bar to support the wings which were not wired.

Figure 60: (left) Flower Bouquet 1. This fan and the next one were inspired by an article that I read. Ladies of the 19th century, when attending a dance, often carried a fan, a dance card and a posy of flowers. A plea was put in for fan makers to produce a fan that resembled a flower posy. Many fan designers tried, but I was not impressed with their results so I decided to attempt it using needlelace flowers. The first one, on abalone shell sticks, was a mixture of painting and lace. When open, painted flowers mingle with needlelace ones and some of these were wired. Both sides of the guard sticks were covered in flowers so that they can be seen from either side and when closed the fan forms a bouquet.

Figure 61 (above): Flower Bouquet 2. This one has much larger needlelace flowers and no painting. The flowers are of no particular variety and are wired with extra petals to give more dimension. I incorporated beads in both leaves and flowers and then assembled them into a bouquet mounted on net. As they were rather large flowers, they are housed on plain wooden sticks.

Figure 62 (left): Madonna and Child — the Holly and the Ivy. Every year, I endeavour to produce a Christmas fan that I can reproduce as a Christmas card. Some can be seen in earlier figures. The Madonna was a challenge to produce a design from a piece of grained wood and some ivy leaves. The grain and knots on the wood gave me the impression of a female figure in a long dress holding a baby. With Christmas in mind, I interpreted it as a Madonna. I used the colour of the wood, which changed from cream to shades of brown, and worked this part in bobbin lace in decorated tape (Milanese). I mounted it in a circular ring.

The ivy leaves were worked in wired needlelace, with beads used for the ivy berries. The holly leaves were made in the same way with padded berries. These were attached lightly to the circular frame to make them three-dimensional and then the frame was attached to a turned stick.

Figure 63 (top right): Good King Wenceslas. I took the theme from the carol and made a bobbin background of snow and trees, working in the same way as the fans depicting the seasons. The figures are in needlelace and attached at the end.

Figure 64 (bottom right): While Shepherds Watched. Another carol worked in bobbin lace. The ground was worked out on polar co-ordinated paper to achieve the curved lines and some coloured weavers were used for the shepherds' clothing, with gold for the angel.

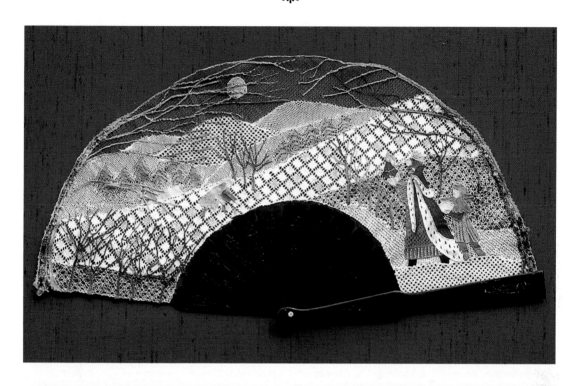

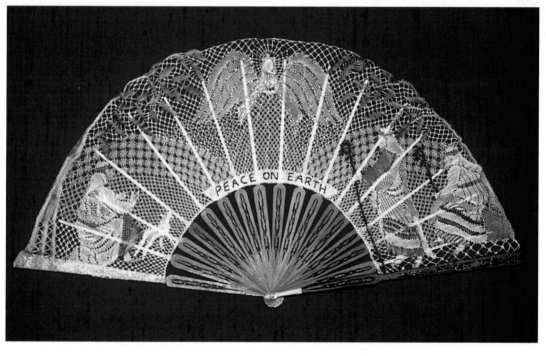

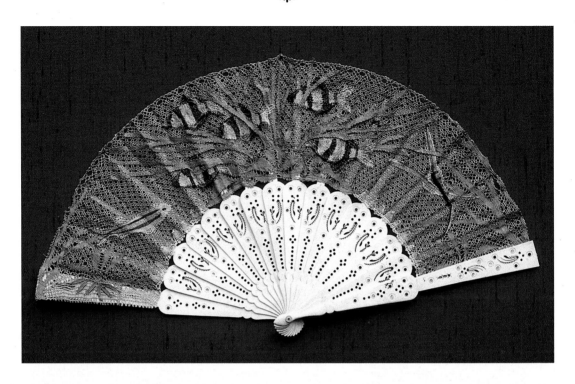

Figure 65 (top left): Under the Sea. This was inspired by underwater scenes on coral reefs. It was worked in bobbin lace in mixed green/blue colours. The tropical fish were made as in Honiton and applied afterwards.

Figure 66 (bottom left): The Little Mermaid. This was worked in bobbin lace, with large holes left in the net sea background to accommodate the swimming mermaids, so that their tails can be seen through the net. The galleon, in needlelace, was also inserted into a hole edged with waves.

Figure 67 (above): Mutiny on the Bounty. This was inspired by a visit to Pitcairn Island where the descendants of Fletcher Christian live. This rocky island has many palm trees and I have depicted the Bounty lying offshore as seen from the island. The needlelace boat is taken from the actual picture of the ship. It is surrounded by fairy terns, which frequent the island. The trees are padded as in stumpwork.

Figure 68 (above): New Zealand North Island. This was made to commemorate a visit. Many of the unique aspects of the island are depicted and worked in a mixture of bobbin lace and needlelace. There are lightly padded kauri trees forming the outer edges, and tree ferns in the dense undergrowth, in which there is a Kiwi. I have included some flax plants from which the Maori skirts are made, and the silver fern used as the national emblem among which are fantails. Steaming White island is off shore with a pohutukawa tree in the foreground. The fan guard sticks were carved in New Zealand by a Maori and are in swamp kauri, 2,000 years old, carbon-dated in Waikato University.

Figure 69 (right): Tree Fern. I was particularly attracted to the tree fern, which is used by the Maoris in their art. They are particularly interested in the fronds as they emerge and begin to grow, and the plant represents a life force. I have used this in the centre of the fan and included a human foetus. This is worked in needlelace, and the actual fern leaves, which are wired, in bobbin lace. It was mounted on an antique stick (from a hand screen) which gave the appearance of the tree trunk.

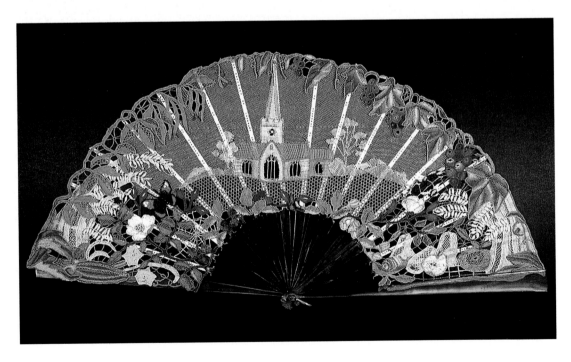

Figure 70 (top left): Carrickmacross in Maori design. I used a typical Maori design, which is employed on many of their decorated textiles. It is black organza on silver net couched in a black thread. When cut away the spaces were filled with the flowers of the kowhai tree. These are the national flowers of New Zealand and are worked in both needlelace and bobbin lace and applied afterwards.

Figure 71 (bottom left): Harvest Festival. This was made in needlelace and bobbin lace to represent the harvest. I wanted to include as many fruits as possible and some of the animals as well as humans who benefit. There are runner beans, grapes, marrows, blackberries, nuts, apples and pears, briar roses and rose hips and sheaves of corn. Animals and insects are eating the fruits and the church is in the misty background. It was worked in bobbin lace in Honiton, Bedfordshire and Bucks techniques with a needlelace surround. It is mounted on antique sticks.

Figure 72 (above) The Pied Piper. This is an illustration of a poem by Robert Browning, with needlelace figures and foreground buildings on a bobbin lace background. There are rats tumbling into the river, and the children gather round the Piper while the townsfolk watch.

Figure 73 (top left): The Canterbury Tales. This was worked in needlelace and bobbin lace and, as in the Pied Piper, the background houses and roadway are in bobbin lace and the foreground houses, Tabard Inn and the figures are in needlelace. I have included the Knight and his Squire, the Widow of Bath. the Miller, the Friar and many others as described by Chaucer, and there are several bystanders. I had worked buildings in bobbin lace in the Pied Piper and these were Bavarian houses; this time they are typically Tudor.

Figure 74 (bottom left): A Midsummer Night's Dream. This was worked entirely in needlelace and mounted on net. The two sets of lovers, Hermia and Lysander and Helena and Demetrius, are at the edges under the trees. Titania lies asleep on the bank and Puck, Cobweb, Mustardseed, Moth and Peaseblossom are sitting in the surrounding trees.

Figure 75 (above): The Highwayman. This was worked in needlelace on a background of darned net (Limerick). This depicts my favourite poem, by Alfred Noyes, which tells the story of a highwayman who visits his love at night and tells her that he will come to her the next night by moonlight. The conversation is heard by Tim the ostler, who calls the soldiers. They tie her up with a gun at her breast and then they wait. She hears him coming and the only way that she can warn him is by firing the gun, which kills her. He escapes but hears of her death in the village the next day and comes back in a frenzy; the soldiers shoot him down and so it ends.

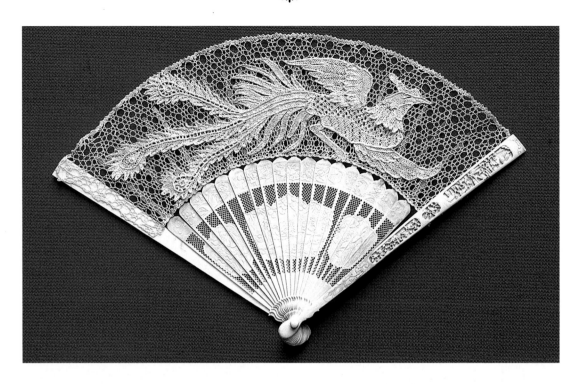

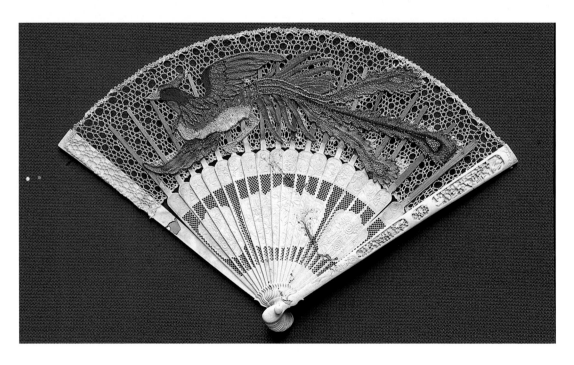

Figures 76 and 77 (left): Double-sided fan. This was made in needlelace on a bobbin lace ground. One side has a coloured Phoenix and the other side a cream Phoenix. It is mounted on double-sided antique sticks.

Figure 78 (above): Nursery Rhymes. This was made with children in mind and I have tried to include as many nursery rhymes as possible. As a design it is too 'busy' but it was fun to do. It was worked in needlelace in a variety of threads and then mounted on net which was darned (Limerick). There are 23 nursery rhymes, including Little Jack Horner, Little Bo-peep, Little Miss Muffet and Ladybird, Ladybird.

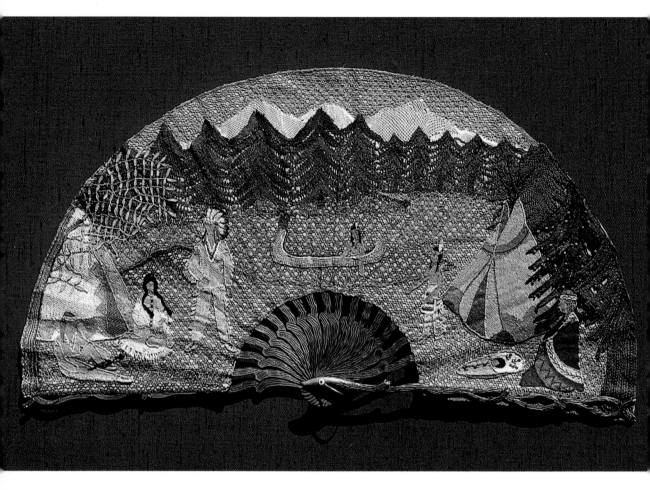

Figure 79: Hiawatha. The poem by Longfellow interested me and I decided to illustrate it. I have taken Hiawatha's life from a papoose by the wigwam of his Grandmother, boating on the lake with his friend Ajidamo (the squirrel) growing up and travelling to another area to meet Minnehaha. The figures and wigwams are in needlelace with the background of water and trees in bobbin lace. The antique sticks were ideal.

Figure 80: The Duck shoot. This was made in bobbin lace with needlelace figures. The idea came from a picture glimpsed in an inn. I drew what I could remember, so it is not the same as the original.

THE LANGUAGE OF THE FAN

In an antique fan box I found a small booklet produced by the Parisian fan maker J. Duvelleroy, and it made interesting reading.

Fans were obviously used widely, particularly in the 17th, 18th and 19th centuries, as a method of communication whose use was taught at many a finishing school.

From reading the booklet, all was geared to love and romance.

It would seem likely that a potential lover would be able to detect from the messages whether his advances were welcome. It seems very odd today but this was an age when it was not 'seemly' to be alone with a man to whom you had not been introduced and anyway you were usually accompanied by a chaperone.

The opportunities for young people to meet one another were limited, so a ballroom was an ideal place to begin a relationship.

First you had to draw attention to yourself by a rapid and noisy shutting of the fan, hoping that this would attract the attention of one with whom you wished to communicate. The fan was then laid down while a curl was adjusted and the reaction observed, then the messages could begin.

Obviously the men had to know all the fan movements too, so maybe they had a book as well.

Fan Movements	Meaning
Carrying the fan in front of the face	Follow me
Carrying in the left hand in front of the face	Desirous of acquaintance
Placing on the left ear	I wish to get rid of you
Drawing across the forehead	You have changed
Twirling in the left hand	We are being watched
Twirling in the right hand	I love another
Carrying in the right hand	You are too willing
Drawing through the hand	I hate you
Drawing across the cheek	I love you
Presented shut	Do you love me?
Drawing across the eyes	I am sorry
Touching the tip with the finger	I wish to speak to you
Letting it rest on the right cheek	Yes
Letting it rest on the left cheek	No
Open and shut	You are cruel
Dropping it	We will be friends
Fanning slowly	I am married
Fanning quickly	I am engaged
With handle to lips	Kiss me
Open wide	Wait for me
Carrying in the left hand open	Come and talk to me
Placing behind the head	Don't forget me
Shut fan resting on the right eye	When can I see you?
Presenting a number of sticks of the fan open	At what hour?
Pressing the half-open fan to the lips	You may kiss me
Covering the left ear with the open fan	Do not betray our secret
Shutting the fully opened fan very slowly	I promise to marry you

Various other movements of the fan were sometimes used to give letters of the alphabet, so that a more detailed conversation was possible. Something akin to the text messaging of today!

GLOSSARY OF TERMS

Abalone	A deep cream mother-of-pearl.
Appliqué	One piece of material applied to another with firm stitches.
Bedfordshire lace	Consists of plaited grounds with leaves and woven trails.
Bobbin lace	Lace made of threads attached to bobbins
Bobbins	Decorated wooden sticks on which the thread is wound for bobbin lace.
Bucks (Buckinghamshire Lace)	A one-piece bobbin lace with a twisted net ground and cloth stitch motifs surrounded with a gimp.
Bullion knots	Long looped stitches made by winding the thread round the needle several times and pulling the needle through.
Buttonhole stitch	Commonly used to describe the stitch for needlelace.
Carrickmacross	Lace made from appliquéd material on net.
Cloth stitch	A term used for the weaving movement in bobbin lace.
Couching	When a thread or threads are held down by another oversewing them.
Couching thread	Fine thread used for couching down a laid thread.
Couronnes	Buttonholed rings worked separately and attached to needlelace.
Darning	Weaving under and over another set of threads, i.e. net.
Edge stitching	A word used for the final buttonholed edge on needlelace (Cordonnet).
Fan sticks	The framework on which a folding fan leaf is attached.
Fillings	Term used to describe the fancy stitches used in all lace.
Gimp	The thicker thread used to outline some bobbin laces, laid between the twists of the ground.
Graph paper	Term used for a squared paper used by lace makers for making net grids.
Ground	Term used to describe the background net of bobbin and needlelace.
Guards	The outer sticks of a fan which are stronger than the rest.
Hand screen	A rigid fan, often shield-shaped, of the early 19th century.
Head	The pivot end of a set of fan sticks through which a rivet is inserted.
Honeycomb	Bucks bobbin-lace ground which has six sides like a honeycomb.
Honiton	A lace made of motifs in bobbin lace that join with 'sewings'.
Isometric paper	A graph paper with angles of 60 degrees, used for Bucks grids.
Leaf	A term used for the semi-circle of fabric which unites the sticks of a fan; a term used for the woven leaf shapes in Bedfordshire and Maltese lace.
Limerick	A lace made by darning on net in various patterns.
Mayflower	A Bucks bobbin-lace stitch formed with small blocks of cloth stitch in a honeycomb ground.
Milanese	A decorated bobbin-lace braid.
Mother-of-pearl	The inside part of a tropical mussel shell.
Needlelace	Lace constructed of buttonhole stitches.
Needlerun	A term often used for the darning stitches in Limerick lace.
Outlining	Word used for the laid thread used in the early stages of needlelace (Fil de Trace).
Passives	Bobbin threads that lie as warp threads in a woven area.
Picots	A term used for the small protrusions added to bars and

	edges in needlelace, also to the twists on the edges of Bucks bobbin lace and sometimes to the looped edge of Carrickmacross.		bobbins.
Pillow	A firmly packed straw cushion on which bobbin lace is made.	Spider	Term used in bobbin lace for the meeting of several threads in a space. It forms the appearance of the legs and body of a spider.
Point ground	The twisted net used in Bucks bobbin lace.	Stick fan	A fixed shape on a single stick similar to a hand screen.
Polar graph paper	Graph paper with a circular grid.	Stumpwork	Padded needlelace dating from the 16th century.
Rivets	The metal pin which holds the fan sticks together at the head.	Tally	Term used for a bobbin lace square made with two pairs of bobbins.
Sewings	Name used for the joining of the piece of one lace to another by taking the weaving thread through the loop on the other side.	Torchon	Bobbin lace in geometric form with a ground at 90˚.
		Tortoiseshell	Shell taken from the Hawkbill turtle, often made into fan sticks.
Spangles	Term used for the metal sequins used to decorate fans from 1750 onwards; also refers to the beads that are attached to	Weavers	A pair of threads used in bobbin lace for weaving solid areas.
		Whipping	Oversewing or overcasting.

L A C E F A N S

BIBLIOGRAPHY

A Collector's Guide to Fans, Bertha de Vere Green:
  Frederick Muller Ltd., 1975
A Collector's History of Fans, Nancy Armstrong:
  Studio Vista, 1974
The Book of Fans, Nancy Armstrong: Colour Library
  International, 1975

FURTHER READING

Treasury of Chinese Motifs, EV Gillon: Dover
  Publications
Treasury of Design for Artists and Craftsmen: Dover
  Publications, 1969
Designs and Patterns for Embroiderers and Craftsmen:
  Dover Publications, 1974
Floral Stained Glass Window Pattern Book, E Sibbett:
  Dover Publications
House of Tours (stained glass), J Miller

SUPPLIERS AND SOURCES OF INFORMATION

UNITED KINGDOM AND REPUBLIC OF IRELAND

GENERAL SUPPLIERS

Alby Lace Museum
Cromer Road
Alby
Norfolk
NR11 7QE

Busy Bobbins
Unit 7
Scarrots lane
Newport
Isle of Wight
PO30 1JD

Chosen Crafts Centre
46 Winchcombe Street
Cheltenham
Gloucestershire
GL52 2ND

Jo Firth
Lace Marketing &
Needlecraft Supplies
58 Kent Crescent
Lowton
Pudsey
West Yorkshire
LS28 9EB

J & J Ford
October hill
Upper Way
Upper Longdon
Rugeley
Staffordshire
WS15 1QB

Doreen Gill
14 Barnfield Road
Petersfield
Hampshire
GU31 4DQ

R Gravestock
Highwood
Crews Hill
Alfrick
Worcestershire
WR6 5HF

The Handicraft Shop
47 Northgate
Canterbury
Kent
CT1 1BE

Frank Herring & Sons
27 High West Street
Dorchester
Dorset
DT1 1UP

Honiton Lace Shop
44 High Street
Honiton
Devon

D J Hornsby
25 Manwood Avenue
Canterbury
Kent
CT2 7AH

Frances Iles
73 High Street
Rochester
Kent
ME1 1LX

Jane's Pincushions
Unit 4
Taverham Crafts
Taverham Nursery Centre
Fir Covent Road
Taverham
Norwich
NR8 6HT

Loricraft
19 Peregrine Way
Grove
Wantage
Oxfordshire
OX12 0QB

Needlestyle
5 The Woolmead
Farnham
Surrey
GU9 7TX

Needlestyle
24–26 West Street
Alresford
Hampshire
SO24 9AT

Needlework
Ann Bartlee
Bucklers Farm
Coggeshall
Essex
CO6 1SB

Needle and Thread
80 High Street
Horsell
Woking
Surrey
GU21 4SZ

The Needlewoman
21 Needless Alley
off New Street
Birmingham
B2 5AE

T Parker
124 Corhampton Road
Boscombe East
Bournemouth
Dorset
BH6 5NZ

Jane Playford
North Lodge
Church Close
West Runton
Norfolk
NR27 9QY

Redburn Crafts
Squires Garden Centre
Halliford Road
Upper Halliford
Shepperton
Middlesex
TW17 8RU

Christine Riley
53 Barclay Street
Stonehaven
Kincardineshire
Scotland
AB39 2AR

Peter & Beverley Scarlett
Strupak
Hill Head
Cold Wells
Ellon
Grampian
Scotland

Ken & Pat Schultz
134 Wisbech Road

Thornley
Peterborough
PE6 0SE

J S Sear
Lacecraft Supplies
8 Hill View
Sherrington
Buckinghamshire
MK16 9NY

Seblace
Waterloo Mills
Howden Road
Silsden
West Yorkshire
RD2 0NA

Shireburn Lace
Finkle Court
Finkle Hill
Sherburn in Elmet
North Yorkshire
LS25 6EB

SMP
4 Garners Close
Chalfont St Peter
Buckinghamshire
SL9 0HB

Southern Handicrafts
20 Kensington Gardens
Brighton
Sussex
BN1 4AC

Spangles
Carole Morris
Burwell
Cambrgeshire
CB5 0ED

Stitches
Dovehouse Shopping
Parade
Warwick Road
Olton
Solihull
West Midlands

Teazle Embroideries
35 Boothferry Road
Hull
North Humberside

Valley house Crafts
Studios
Ruston

Scarborough
North Yorkshire
George Walker
The Corner Shop
Rickinghall
Diss
Norfolk

BOBBINS

A R Arches
The poplars
Shetland
Near Stowmarket
Suffolk
IP14 3DE

T Brown
Temple Lane Cottage
Littledean
Cinderford
Gloucestershire

Chrisken Bobbins
26 Cedar Drive
Kingsclere
Buckinghamshire
RG15 8TD

Malcolm J Fielding
2 Northern Terrace
Moss Lane
Silverdale
Lancahire
LA5 0ST

R Gravestock
Highwood
Crews Hill
Alfrick
Worcestershire
WR6 5HF

Loricraft
19 Peregrine Way
Grove
Wantage
Oxfordshire

T parker
124 Corhampton Road
Boscombe East
Bornemouth
Dorset
BH6 5NZ

Bryan Philips
Pantglas
Cellan
Lampeter
Dyfed
SA48 8JD

D H Shaw
47 Lamor Crescent
Thrushcroft
Rotherham
South Yorkshire
S66 9QD

Sizelands
1 Highfield Road
Winslow
Buckinghamshire
MK10 3QU

Richard Viney
Unit 7
Port Royal Street
Southsea
Hampshire
PO5 3UD

GEMSTONES AND JEWELLERY FINDINGS

Gaycharm Ltd
(mail order)
168 Chadwell Heath
Road
Romford
Essex
RM6 6HT

GOLD THREADS AND FINE WIRE

Stephen Simpson
(mail order)
Avenham Road Works
Preston
Lancashire

FAN STICKS

Malcolm Cox
Howth Woodcrafts
Gwynfa Bach
Thormanby Road
Howth
Co. Dublin
Rep. of Ireland

NETS

Romance Bridals
(mail order)
12 D'Arblay Street
London
W1F 8DU

BOOKS

Christopher Williams
19 Morrison Avenue
Parkstone
Poole
Dorset
BH17 4AD

SILK EMBROIDERY AND LACE THREADS

E & J Piper
Silverlea
Flax Lane
Glemsford
Suffolk
CO10 7RS

SILK WEAVING YARN

Hilary Chetwynd
Kipping Cottage
Cheriton
Alresford
Hampshire
SO24 0PW

FRAMES AND MOUNTS

Doreen Campbell
Highcliff
Brenisham Road
Malmesbury
Wiltshire

MATT COLOURED TRANSPARENT ADHESIVE FILM

Heffers Craphic Shop
26 King Street
Cmbridge
CB1 1LN

LINEN BY THE METRE (YARD) AND MADE UP ARTICLES OF CHURCH LINEN

Mary Collins
Church Furnishings
St Andrews Hall
Humber Doucy Lane
Ipswich
Suffolk
IP4 3BP

Hayes & Finch
Head Office & Factory
Hanson Road
Aintree
Liverpool
L9 9BP

General Suppliers
Overseas

UNITED STATES OF AMERICA

Arbor house
22 Arbor Lane
Roslyn Hights
NY11577

Baltazor Inc.
3262 Severn Avenue
Metairie
LA 7002

Beggars' Lace
PO Box 17263
Denver
Colorado 80217

Berga Ullman Inc.
PO Box 918
North Adams
Massachusetts 01247

Frederick J Fawcett
129 South Street
Boston
Massachusetts 02130

Frivolité
15526 Densmore N.
Seattle
Washington 98113

Happy Hands
3007 SW Marshall
Pendleton
Oregon 97180

International Old Lacers
PO Box 1029
Westminster
Colorado 80030

Lace Place de Belgique
800 SW 17th Street
Boca Raton
FL 33432

Lacis
2150 Stuart Street
Berkeley
California 9470

Robin's Bobbins
RTL Box 1736
Mineral Bluff
Georgia 30559

Robin and Russ
Handweavers
533 North Adams Street
McMinnvills
Oregon 97128

Some Place
2990 Adline Street
Berkeley
California 94703

Osma G Todd Studio
319 Mendoza Avenue
Coral Gables
Florida 33134

The Unique And Art
Lace Cleaners
5926 Delman Boulevard
St Louis
Missouri 63112

Van Scriver Bobbin Lace
130 Cascadilla park
Ithaca
New York 14850

The World in Stitches
82 South Street
milford
NH 03055

AUSTRALIA

Dentelles Lace Supplies
3 Narrak Close
Jindalee
Queensland 4074
The Lacemaker
94 Forham Avenue
Hartwell
Victoria 3124

Spindle and Loom
Arcade 83
Longueville road
Lane cove
NSW 2066

Tulis Crafts
201 Avoca Street
Randwick
NSW 2031

BELGIUM

't Handwekhuisje
Katelijnestraat 23
8000 Bruges

Kantcentrum
Balstraat 14
8000 Bruges

Manufacture Belge de
Dentelle
6 Galerie de la Reine
Galeries Royales St
Hubert
1000 Bruxelles

Orchidee
Mariastraat 18
8000 Bruges

Ann Thys
't Apostelientje
Balstraat 11
8000 Bruges

FRANCE

Centre d'Initiations à la
Dentelle du Puy
2 Rue Duguesclin
43000 Le Puy en Velay

A L'Econome
Anne-Marie Deydier
Ecole de Dentelle aux
Fuseaux
10 rue Paul Chenavard
69001 Lyon

Rougier and Ple
13–15 bd des Filles de
Calvaire
75003 Paris

GERMANY

Der Fenster laden
Beliner Str. 8
D 6483 Bad Soden
Salmunster

P P Hempel
Orolanweg 34
1000 Berlin 47

Heikona De Ruijter
Kleoppelgrosshandel
Langer Steinweg 38
D4933 Blomberg

HOLLAND

Blokker's Boektiek
Bronsteeweg 4/4a
2101 AC Heemstede

Theo Brejaat
Postbus 5199
3008 Ad Rotterdam

Magazijn De Vlijt
Lijnmarkt 48
Utrecht

SWITZERLAND

Fadehax
Inh. Irene Solca
4105 Biel-Benken
Basel

NEW ZEALAND

Peter mcLeavey
PO Box 69.007
Auckland 8

SOURCES OF
INFORMATION

The Lace Guild
The Hollies
53 Audnam
Stourbridge
West Midlands
DY8 4AE

The Lacemakers' Circle
49 Wardwick
Derby
DE1 1HY

The Lace society
Linwood
Stratford Road
Oversley
Alcester
Warwickshire
BY9 6PG

International Old Lacers
S Hurst
4 Dollius Road
London
N3 1RG

The Fan Museum
12 Crooms Hill
Greenwich
London
SE10 8ER

Fan Circle International
Secretary: Mrs J Milligan
Cronk-y-Voddy
Rectory road
Coltishall
Norwich
NR12 7HF

INDEX